NO LONGER —YOUR— DOORMAT

A Practical Guide to Releasing Doormat Behaviors

Updated Edition

Renee A. Gibbons

Contents

Acknowledgments

To my beloved husband, William—

Your unwavering support, quiet strength, and steadfast belief in me carried this book from vision to reality. Words fall short of expressing the depth of my gratitude. Thank you for walking beside me every step of the way.

To LaGayle and Weiner—

Your early encouragement planted the seed. Your faith in my voice gave me the courage to bring this book to fruition.

To Dr. Jermaine—

Thank you for generously sharing your powerful story of healing. Your voice adds depth, truth, and hope to these pages.

To the Readers—

Thank you for your courage. By picking up this book, you've taken a powerful step toward reclaiming your voice, your worth, and your peace. Whether you're just beginning to recognize the patterns that have held you back or you're deep in the work of healing, know this: you are not alone. Your story matters. Your boundaries matter. I wrote these pages with you in mind, and I pray they serve as a mirror, a map, and a companion on your journey to wholeness. Keep going. You are worthy of a life rooted in dignity, clarity, and love.

Why I Wrote This Book

I AM A REFORMED DOORMAT. Being a "doormat" for decades is a characterization I did not choose or want. However, it is the best term to capture my decades of silence or shrinking when disrespected. It best captures how I let mistreatment slide over and over again. Behaviors that pushed me to the brink of emotional exhaustion and nearly broke me. Behaviors that, if I had not changed, would have had insurmountable and generational consequences.

For years, I blamed others for disrespecting and mistreating me until a painful realization: the common denominator in every toxic relationship was me. I NEVER set standards for how I should be treated. I NEVER shut it down when those standards were crossed.

This book was born from that breaking point and the powerful transformation that followed.

Maybe you are reading this book because you're tired too. Maybe you're trying to navigate relationships—at home, at work, or even in your own family—where you feel disrespected or dismissed. Maybe you're searching for answers, for a way to speak up, set boundaries, and stop tolerating what hurts you.

I wrote *"No Longer Your Doormat"* for you—to share what I've learned through years of reflection, healing, and courageous change. I wrote it with a heartfelt desire to offer solutions to those of you who need something different in your relationships.

Today, I can effectively shut down disrespect without guilt. I speak and walk with confidence. I show up as my full, authentic self. And I value myself more than I value anyone's approval. I want that freedom for you, also.

You Are Not Alone

Doormat behavior is more common than people admit. Many of us—women and men—walk on eggshells, swallow our feelings, and put up with emotional harm. We do this because we don't know how to handle toxic behavior. And it happens everywhere: in families, friendships, partner or spousal relationships, and yes, even at work.

You see, we live in a world where disrespect gets brushed off as "that's just how he or she is." Cruelty is often disguised as "being honest." When this behavior is normalized, it's easy to start doubting yourself. You wonder if you're overreacting. You wonder if you should just keep the peace. You wonder if speaking up will make things worse.

In the workplace, doormat behavior and burnout often go hand in hand. It is the place where burnout doesn't just come from long hours or heavy workloads. It comes from constantly saying yes when you're already overextended, taking on responsibilities that aren't yours, or absorbing other people's toxicity.

Burnout slowly drains your energy because you keep pushing yourself past your limits while pretending everything is fine. It wears you down emotionally, especially if you are the dependable one, the fixer, and the one who never complains.

However, you're not alone. You are not the only one:

- who struggles to say "no."
- who feels disrespected again and again.

- who doesn't know how to shut down bad behavior.
- who carries more than your share because you don't want to rock the boat.

Waiting for others to change won't fix the problem. Toxic patterns don't magically disappear. Workplaces don't suddenly become healthy. People don't wake up one day and decide to treat you better just because you've been patient.

Real change begins when you start showing up differently. When you decide your voice matters. When you choose boundaries over burnout. When you stop shrinking and start standing.

How This Book Can Help You

This is not a book about how to fix other people. It's about transforming the one person you can control: *yourself.*

This book will walk beside you through this shift. To remind you that you're not powerless. You can reclaim your voice. You can protect your peace. You can shape how you show up in every relationship—including the one you have with yourself.

And it all starts with one simple truth: You deserve more than burnout. You deserve more than silence. You deserve more than being anyone's doormat.

The six actions outlined in this book helped me shift my doormat behaviors, assert my voice, and build relationships rooted in respect, authenticity, and emotional balance. These actions are not quick fixes. They are mindset shifts—practices that require courage, consistency, and self-compassion.

Here's what you'll gain:

- **Clarity:** You'll learn to identify toxic patterns—both in others and in yourself.

- **Boundaries**: You'll discover how to implement boundaries without guilt or fear.

- **Courage:** You'll explore ways to speak up, even when your voice shakes.

- **Self-awareness:** You'll examine your own behaviors and beliefs that may be keeping you stuck.

- **Growth:** You'll understand how to reshape your mindset and confidence from the inside out.

- **Language:** You'll learn ways to communicate your needs with authenticity and emotional integrity.

Important Note:

This book focuses on releasing doormat behaviors to effectively shut down emotional and psychological relationship patterns that can be toxic in relationships. It does not address physical abuse. If you are experiencing physical harm, your safety is the priority. The most important step is to remove yourself from danger and seek support from professionals who are trained to help.

What's Ahead

In the Chapters ahead, you'll explore:

- What does doormat behavior look like?

- Why do we fall into these patterns?

- How do we break free to a place of authenticity, confidence, and peace?

Chapter Three will help you assess your own behavior, and the rest of the book will guide you through practical steps to reshape your relationships. You'll find self-reflection questions and activities throughout to help you delve deeper and apply what you've learned.

This journey is personal, powerful, and possible. So, are you ready to begin?

Chapter One

What is a Doormat?

Let's take a deeper dive into this term together. The word "doormat" is a metaphor to describe certain types of behavior. To understand this pattern, let's start with a vivid image.

Imagine a worn, faded welcome mat at the front door. It's covered in muddy footprints, frayed at the edges, and flattened from years of being stepped on. It never resists. It never speaks. It simply absorbs whatever is dragged across it.

Now imagine that the "doormat" is a person.

- They absorb whatever is thrown at them.

- They allow others to walk all over their boundaries.

- They endure being trampled emotionally, mentally, and sometimes spiritually.

- They become a dumping ground for other people's negativity, disrespect, and abuse.

This metaphor captures a behavioral pattern that many people fall into—often without realizing it.

Doormat Moments You Might Recognize

Doormat behavior doesn't start with big, confrontational events. It begins with small slights and disrespectful incidents where you swallow your truth, silence your discomfort, or decide your needs can wait.

Picture these incidents:

- You are in a meeting, and someone interrupts you for the third time. You feel the sting of their rudeness, but you smile politely and let it go.
- A family member makes cruel, cutting remarks about you to other family members. You laugh it off even though it hurts.
- A friend asks for yet another favor, and even though you're exhausted, you say yes.

None of these incidents seems big on their own. But over time, they add up.

They shape a pattern.

They shape a life.

This was my life for an exceptionally long time.

The Reality of Doormat Behavior

People who operate as doormats often:

- accept mistreatment without protest.

- suppress their own needs to accommodate others.

- tolerate verbal and emotional abuse, including:
  - yelling and name-calling,
  - gaslighting and manipulation,
  - degrading comments and gameplaying.

Doormat behaviors do not come from weakness. They are patterns that slowly take root, often long before you notice how much they're costing you.

How Do You Describe Doormat Behavior?

Here are some descriptive words I've come up with to capture this pattern.

- people-pleasing

- over-accommodating

- self-effacing

- non-assertive

- overly agreeable

- obsequious

- yielding

Here are some additional colorful expressions people often use:

- letting people walk all over you

- always taking the back seat

- bending over backwards

- handing over the steering wheel of your life

- being everyone's yes-man or yes-woman

- carrying other people's baggage

- being the office or family dumping ground

- always eating last at the table

- holding the door but never walking through it

- playing the background character in your own story

These traits aren't inherently bad. Many of them come from kindness, empathy, or a desire to keep the peace. But when they consistently override your own needs and leave you feeling depleted or resentful, it's time to take a closer look.

Why Doormat Behavior Is a Problem

Many people do not see themselves as doormats. They see themselves as kind, generous, or patient. But when these well-meaning behaviors consistently cost you your peace, dignity, or emotional well-being, it becomes self-erasure.

You may say things like:

- "I'm just accepting them the way they are."

- "That's just how they talk."

- "It's not worth the argument."

Meanwhile, every interaction with that person leaves you feeling smaller, drained, or quietly resentful.

Doormat behavior, especially when paired with toxic relationship patterns:

- strips away your self-respect.

- dismantles healthy boundaries.

- invites exploitation of your kindness.

- silences your voice and suppresses your needs.

- breeds resentment and emotional exhaustion.

- disconnects you from your own worth.

In trying to please everyone, you risk losing the most important relationship you have: the one with yourself.

Why Doormat Behavior Patterns Persist

Doormat behavior persists because something inside you prevents you from challenging toxic or disrespectful actions.

When you don't speak up, set boundaries, or walk away from mistreatment, you unintentionally teach others how to treat you. The offender keeps behaving the same way because they've learned there will be:

- no pushback.

- no consequences.

- no shift in the dynamic.

And when nothing changes, nothing changes.

Over time, this becomes a predictable loop:

- Silence invites mistreatment.

- Mistreatment reinforces silence.

- The cycle repeats until something breaks.

These patterns can last for years—in families, friendships, partner or spousal relationships, and especially in workplaces where power imbalances and burnout make it even harder to speak up.

The Good News

No matter how long you've been stuck in these patterns, you are not powerless. You are not broken. And you are not destined to stay this way.

Change begins the moment you decide your voice matters. It begins the moment you choose to honor your worth. It begins the moment you say, *"No more."*

You can interrupt toxic cycles that feel unshakeable. You can establish boundaries that protect your peace, your dignity, and your emotional well-being.

You can learn to show up in your personal and professional relationships with confidence and clarity—rooted in self-respect, authenticity, and emotional strength.

This transformation doesn't require perfection. It requires awareness, courage, and a willingness to try something different. Even small shifts—speaking up once, saying no once, choosing yourself once—begin to rewrite the script.

Before we dive into how to break free, let's take a closer look at **why** people become doormats in the first place. Understanding the "why" is the first step toward reclaiming your power and rewriting your story.

Chapter Two

The Doormat Dilemma: Why Are People Doormats?

Take a moment to reflect: Why do people allow themselves to be treated like doormats? What came to mind?

For years, I unknowingly operated as a "doormat" in my relationships. At times, I didn't even recognize toxic and disrespectful behaviors, let alone do anything about them. And when I recognized disrespect or mistreatment, I felt powerless to do anything about it.

A critical first step during my healing came when I asked myself:

"Why was I a doormat? Why didn't I stand up for myself? Why did I allow people to mistreat or disrespect me?"

These were questions I could not answer initially. However, these questions cracked something open in me. They marked the beginning of a deeper understanding about myself—one that led to clarity, healing, and ultimately, freedom.

The Anatomy of a Doormat

Let's dig deeper into the "why" together. Through research, reflection, and experience, I've identified ten patterns that often shape doormat behavior. As you read each one, ask yourself whether any of these patterns show up in your life.

1. **People-Pleasing**: Nearly half of adults identify as people-pleasers. You say yes when you really want to say no. You overextend yourself and neglect your own needs to keep others happy.

Consequences of People-Pleasing

People-pleasers are easily overused and exploited. Once others know you rarely say "no," their requests multiply. Some people genuinely don't realize you're stretched thin. However, others intentionally take advantage of your kindness—draining your time, energy, and emotional reserves.

Example:

Your cousin asks you to watch her kids "just this once," but it becomes every weekend. You're exhausted and resentful, yet you keep saying yes.

2. **Fear of Conflict**: Avoiding confrontation feels safer than risking rejection or anger. You keep the peace, even when it costs you your dignity.

Consequences of Fearing Conflict

When you avoid conflict, you silently accept mistreatment. People learn you won't push back, so the disrespect continues unchecked. Over time, you lose your voice, your boundaries, and your sense of agency. The "peace" you protect becomes a prison.

Example:

Your teenage son routinely speaks to you with a sharp, dismissive tone. Each time it happens, you feel a knot in your stomach, but you tell yourself, "He's stressed. It's just a phase. I don't want to start an argument."

Over time, his disrespect becomes the norm. He interrupts you, ignores your requests, and rolls his eyes when you speak. You stay silent and allow the disrespect to continue.

3. **Low Self-Worth:** When you don't believe you deserve respect, you tolerate disrespect. You stay silent. And that silence speaks volumes about how little you value your own voice.

Consequences of Low Self-Worth

Low self-worth creates self-abandonment. You accept crumbs and let others set the terms of your life. The more you tolerate, the more you believe you're unworthy of better.

Example:

Your partner constantly criticizes you in front of your friends and family members. You laugh it off, even though it hurts, because deep down you believe "this is the best I can get."

4. **Desire to Be Loved**: You equate agreeable-
ness with lovability. You fear that boundaries
will push people away. Saying "yes" becomes a
currency for acceptance.

Consequences of Desire to Be Loved

When love becomes something you must earn
rather than something you deserve, you
overextend yourself emotionally. You tolerate
unhealthy behavior, hoping your sacrifices will
secure affection. Instead, you attract
relationships where your needs are secondary
or ignored entirely.

Example:

You loan money you can't afford to give because
you're afraid your friend will be upset or pull
away if you say no.

5. **Guilt**: Saying no feels selfish. You overextend yourself to ease guilt, often at the expense of your own needs.

Consequences of Guilt

Guilt-driven giving leads to resentment, burnout, and emotional exhaustion. You become responsible for everyone's comfort but your own. And because guilt never truly goes away, you stay trapped in a cycle of overdoing and under-receiving.

Example:

You agree to host a family holiday even though you're overwhelmed, because you feel guilty saying no—especially when "everyone is counting on you."

6. **Lack of Assertiveness Skills**: You do not know how to speak up or stand up for yourself. You weren't taught. You weren't allowed.

Saying "no," asking for what you want, or setting limits feels foreign or intimidating.

Consequences of Lack of Assertiveness Skills

Without assertiveness skills, you default to silence or compliance. Others make decisions for you. Your needs go unmet. You feel invisible, powerless, and overlooked—not because you lack value, but because you lack the tools to express it.

Example:

Your supervisor assigns you extra tasks "because you're so reliable." You accept them without question, even though your workload is already full.

7. **Fear of Abandonment**: You accept mistreatment to avoid being left. You cling to toxic relationships out of fear.

Consequences of Fear of Abandonment

This fear keeps you tethered to people who don't treat you well. You tolerate disrespect, manipulation, or emotional neglect because the thought of being alone feels worse than the pain you're experiencing. Your self-worth becomes tied to someone else's presence.

Example:

Your partner threatens to leave whenever you try to address an issue. To avoid conflict or abandonment, you stop expressing issues altogether.

8. **Over-Identification with the Caregiver Role**: You feel valuable when you're needed, even to the point of self-neglect. Your worth becomes tied to how much you give.

Consequences of Over-Identification with the Caregiver Role

When your identity is built on caring for others, you end up ignoring your own needs. You become overextended, under-supported, and emotionally drained. People begin to rely on you without offering anything in return, creating one-sided relationships.

Example:

You're the "go-to" person for everyone's crises. Even when you're sick or exhausted, you drop everything to help—because you don't know who you are if you're not the helper.

9. **Belief That Suffering Equals Virtue**: Cultural or religious teachings may glorify self-denial. You wear your suffering like a badge of honor, believing it makes you morally superior.

Consequences of Belief that Suffering Equals Virtue

This belief normalizes emotional neglect and unhealthy sacrifice. You begin to equate pain with purpose and endurance with righteousness. As a result, you stay in situations that harm you, believing your suffering is noble or spiritually meaningful.

Example:

You stay in a draining ministry role because you believe "serving others means putting yourself last," even though you're burning out.

10. **Hope That People Will Change**: You stay, you suffer, you wait—believing your loyalty, patience, and kindness will inspire transformation. In doing so, you repeatedly accept poor treatment, justifying it as part of a future payoff.

Consequences of Hoping People will Change

Hope becomes a trap. You invest emotionally in someone's potential instead of their reality. You excuse harmful behavior, minimize red flags, and sacrifice your well-being for a version of the person that may never exist.

Example:

You've been dating someone for two years who keeps promising they'll "do better." They say they'll communicate more, stop disappearing during disagreements, and finally follow through on their commitments. Every time they break a promise, they apologize with just enough emotion to make you believe change is right around the corner.

You cling to the glimpses of who they could be—their charm, their potential, the moments when they're attentive and kind. But those moments are rare, and the disrespect is consistent. Still, you stay, telling yourself, "They're trying," even though their actions never match their words.

Over time, you realize you've built a relationship with their potential, not their reality. And in the process, you've abandoned your own needs, hoping your patience will inspire a transformation that never comes.

When Awareness Becomes Power

When you step back and look at these ten patterns, a powerful truth emerges: no one becomes a doormat because they are weak, foolish, or incapable.

Doormat behavior arises from unmet needs, unhealed wounds, and unconscious habits.

Awareness is the first crack in the armor of old patterns. Once you can name what has shaped you,

you can choose differently. You can reclaim your voice, your boundaries, and your worth. You can rewrite the story you've been living.

This chapter is not an indictment; it's an invitation. An invitation to see yourself with honesty and compassion, to recognize the patterns that no longer serve you, and to step boldly into the freedom that comes when you finally decide: I will no longer be a doormat.

Chapter Three

Am I a Doormat?

This chapter invites you to pause and reflect on your relationships, especially those that leave you feeling mistreated, undervalued, disrespected, or emotionally depleted. There's no judgment here. These questions are designed to help you gain clarity, build self-awareness, and begin asserting your voice and boundaries.

Take your time with each question. Be honest. Your answers are for you. They hold the power to shift your perspective.

Self-Reflection Questions

1. Do you often agree to requests, even when your inner voice is whispering or screaming "no"? What emotions, fears, or beliefs might be driving this response?

2. Do you frequently put others' needs ahead of your own needs? How does this affect your emotional, physical, or mental well-being?

3. When someone disrespects or mistreats you, how do you typically respond or react? What do you do when the same person crosses the line repeatedly?

4. Are there relationships where you consistently give far more than you get? How long have you accepted this imbalance, and what stops you from addressing it?

5. Reflecting on the 10 doormat behaviors (see Chapter 2), which do you see in yourself? List all that apply.

What Do Your Responses Reveal?

Now, take a moment to review your responses. What recurring patterns do you see?

If your answers show that you set boundaries and foster mutual respect—beautiful! Continue walking in confidence and authenticity. You are modeling what a healthy connection looks like.

If your self-reflection responses reveal doormat tendencies you'd like to change, know this: awareness is the beginning of change. Your responses are not a verdict; they're a mirror. And what you see in that mirror is not weakness, but a powerful opportunity to grow.

My Story: From Doormat to Empowered Woman

I grew up in a stable, middle-class home in the 1960s and 1970s with my hard-working mother and stepfather. My mother worked full-time, attended college part-time, and ran a tight ship at home, even when away.

Chores came before play and had to be completed before she got home. Her parenting style reflected the times: children were seen, not heard; respecting authority was mandatory, and questioning it was off-limits.

Our home was orderly and disciplined, not warm or emotionally expressive. Love was demonstrated through responsibility, not affection. There was no space to share feelings or ask "why." In this environment, I learned early that silence was safer than honesty, compliance safer than conflict, and shrinking myself kept the peace. I internalized one lesson: my voice didn't matter.

I carried that belief into adulthood. I, too, tried to emulate the same parenting style, thinking it was the best model to follow. I didn't yet understand how deeply it had shaped my inability to speak up, set boundaries, or advocate for myself.

As a girl, I didn't know how to use my voice—whether it was unfair punishment from nuns, cruelty from classmates, or bullying. I endured instead of resisting. I absorbed instead of expressing. After high school, I joined the military, where obedience was valued over assertiveness. I became a textbook doormat. Yet the military gave me something priceless: resilience. Even in silence, something inside me was strengthening.

At 22, I married—too young and too unaware of myself. My 20s and 30s looked ideal from the outside: a husband, two beautiful children, a home, and engaged parents. We worked hard and lived well.

Motherhood fulfilled me. I loved leading Girl Scouts and found purpose in helping underserved adults through training and career development. Behind closed doors, unresolved toxic relationship patterns destroyed my relationships. My inability to shut down mistreatment and disrespect in my home led to a blatant lack of goodwill toward one another. The toxicity eroded me until I chose silence to keep the peace—a peace that never came.

By age 39, I was shattered, burnt out, and heartbreakingly unhappy.

Then came the turning point.

The Awakening

My 40s were a decade of transformation. I began to recognize the toxic patterns. My marriage ended. My relationship with my mother shifted as

I stopped people-pleasing and started honoring my own needs.

I rebuilt myself—personally, professionally, and spiritually. I returned to college, earned my bachelor's degree, and later a graduate degree just after turning 50. After years of inner work, I met the man who is now my husband, best friend, and partner in growth.

My 50s were a renaissance. I returned to the training and development field, writing and teaching professional and leadership development courses. This career shift deepened my self-awareness. I learned to say "no" with confidence and call out bad behavior respectfully. Some relationships ended, but I forgave myself, let go of the past, and embraced peace.

The Power of Responsibility

In my 60s, I decided to write about my healing and restoration journey. In telling my story, I reached another level of growth—fully understanding that my doormat behaviors played a significant role in my toxic relationship cycles.

This wasn't about self-blame; it was an act of fierce reclamation. I couldn't rewrite the past, but I could reclaim the story I lived and finally become the woman I longed to be.

I'm not an expert. I'm a woman who lived as a doormat. A woman who changed. A woman who can now tell her story as it deserves to be told— with clarity, courage, and compassion.

Your Turn

If you see yourself in my story, know this: you can change, too. You have the power to rediscover your voice, honor your worth, and protect your boundaries. You are not anyone's doormat, and you never have to be again.

Now that you can see the habits, fears, and beliefs that may be keeping you stuck in "doormat" behavior patterns, the next step is far more powerful: transforming them. The following chapters will help you do just that.

Chapter Four

Introduction: Six Actions to Release Doormat Behaviors

In the following chapters, we'll explore six actions that helped me recognize toxic relationship patterns, establish healthy boundaries, and release my doormat behaviors with both confidence and compassion.

Action #1: Identify Toxic Relationship Patterns

Action #2: Seek Clarity and Support

Action #3: Implement Boundaries and Consequences with Clarity and Confidence

Action #4: Know Yourself and Grow Yourself

Action #5: Determine How or If the Relationship Can Continue

Action #6: Restoration and Healing: Say Goodbye to Doormat Behaviors

These actions didn't just shift how I interacted with others; they reshaped how I saw myself. Each one invites you to step into greater self-awareness, courage, and emotional honesty as you build a life where your voice, needs, and dignity are honored.

Releasing doormat behaviors is not a passive process. It takes real work—consistent, courageous, internal work. You will be asked to examine long-standing habits, challenge beliefs that once felt like truth, and practice new behaviors that may feel uncomfortable in the beginning. This transformation doesn't happen by wishing for change; it happens by showing up for yourself day after day, even when the steps feel small or slow. The work is worth it because you are worth it.

And let's be honest, there will be missteps along the way. You may slip back into old patterns, hesitate when you meant to speak up, or set a boundary only to soften it later. That doesn't mean you've failed. It means you're human. Growth is rarely a straight line. Every misstep is simply an invitation to try again with more clarity, more strength, and more self-compassion. The goal is progress, not perfection.

As you move through these six actions, I encourage you to stay open, stay patient, and stay committed to your own healing. You are stepping into a new way of being—one rooted in dignity, authenticity, and emotional freedom. This journey will challenge you, but it will also empower you in ways you may not yet imagine. And by the time you reach the other side, you'll recognize the strength that has been inside you all along.

Let's walk through your growth journey together!

Chapter Five

Action #1: Identify Toxic Relationship Patterns

Disrespect and mistreatment aren't always loud and dramatic. Sometimes they slip in quietly through sarcasm, silence, dismissive comments, or subtle control. These behaviors can show up anywhere: in families, friendships, workplaces, and partner or spousal relationships.

Not every slight or misunderstanding requires confrontation. But when harmful patterns become chronic—draining your energy, chipping away at your confidence, or leaving you emotionally unsettled—they deserve your attention.

Identifying toxic relationship patterns is not about pointing fingers. It's about activating your power, protecting your peace, and shifting relationship dynamics to honor your worth. It's also about seeing yourself clearly to determine if you are also engaging in toxic behaviors.

My Wake-Up Call

For years, I was naïve to toxic patterns in my relationships. I genuinely believed that most people had good motives or intentions towards me, especially if they were my friend, family member, or significant other. I also did not see blind spots in myself that were contributing to toxic relationship patterns.

It took growth, painful experiences, and a lot of self-reflection to realize that not everyone had good intentions. Some people were unaware of their toxic behaviors. Others were fully aware and benefited from my silence and inability to stand up for myself.

I didn't have the language for what I was experiencing. I just knew something felt "off," but I blamed myself instead of questioning the pattern.

Identifying toxic behaviors was the first major step in releasing my doormat tendencies. It helped me see that my pain wasn't imaginary, my boundaries weren't unreasonable, and my voice mattered. I want the same clarity for you.

This chapter outlines **twelve common toxic relationship patterns**. For each one, you'll find:

- a clear definition.

- a real-world example.

- the emotional and psychological impact.

These patterns often overlap, and this list is not exhaustive—but it serves as a powerful starting point. As you read, pause to reflect:

- Have I experienced this?
- Have I tolerated this?
- Have I normalized this?
- Have I internalized this?

Use the self-reflection questions in this chapter to document toxic relationship patterns that show up in your relationships.

Later in this chapter, we'll also explore generational toxic behavior patterns that didn't start with you but were handed down through family norms, unspoken rules, and survival strategies. As you move into this section, I invite you to reflect honestly to determine if you recognize behaviors that have been present in your family for decades.

Awareness isn't about blame; it's about breaking cycles and choosing a healthier path forward.

12 Common Toxic Relationship Patterns

1. Disrespecting One's Personal Space

Definition: Ignoring or violating physical, emotional, or psychological boundaries—whether through unwanted touch, invading privacy, or dismissing requests for space.

Example:

You've made it clear to a co-worker that you are not interested romantically. Yet they show up uninvited at your desk and rub your shoulders.

Detrimental Impact:

Boundary violations create discomfort, anxiety, and a sense of being unsafe. Over time, they erode trust and make you question whether your needs matter. You may begin shrinking yourself to avoid conflict or discomfort.

2. Passive-Aggressiveness

Definition: Expressing hostility or resentment indirectly, often through sarcasm, procrastination, sabotage, or subtle digs, rather than through honest communication.

Example:

You and a co-worker have worked closely on a project for over a year. After disagreeing with you in a meeting, they exclude you from essential project emails.

Detrimental Impact:

Passive-aggressive behavior creates confusion and emotional instability. You're left trying to decode hidden messages instead of engaging in healthy dialogue. It undermines trust, creates a hostile environment, and fosters resentment.

3. **Condescending**

Definition: Acting superior through belittling comments, patronizing tones, expressing disdain, or by dismissing someone's thoughts, feelings, or accomplishments.

Example:

At family functions, your sibling talks down to you and constantly belittles you in front of everyone, especially when you talk about the positive things happening in your life.

Detrimental Impact:

Condescension creates a power imbalance in the relationship and chips away at your confidence and self-esteem. It creates an emotional hierarchy in which your voice is minimized, and theirs is elevated. Over time, you may begin doubting your abilities.

4. **Verbal Abuse**

Definition: Using words to hurt, intimidate, or control—through yelling, name-calling, threats, or humiliation.

Example:

During an argument, your partner screams, "You're worthless! No one else would ever want you." These verbal outbursts occur regularly.

Detrimental Impact:

Verbal abuse leaves deep emotional scars that linger long after the words fade. It creates fear, shame, and emotional instability. You may begin to believe the insults, which damage your self-worth.

5. **Gaslighting**

Definition: Deliberately manipulating someone into doubting their memory, perception, or sanity.

Example:

Your friend frequently cancels plans. When you confront them, they insist it only happened once and claim you were lying about additional cancellations.

Detrimental Impact:

Gaslighting destabilizes your sense of reality. You begin questioning your judgment, your memory, and even your emotional responses. This creates dependency and erodes your confidence.

6. **Blame Shifting**

Definition: Redirecting responsibility onto others, even when clearly at fault.

Example:

Your partner forgets your birthday, then says, "Well, you didn't remind me. You know how busy I am."

Detrimental Impact:

Blame shifting creates emotional exhaustion. You end up apologizing for things you didn't do and carrying guilt that isn't yours. It prevents accountability and healthy conflict resolution.

7. **One-Sided Pattern**

Definition: A dynamic where one person consistently gives, sacrifices, or compromises while the other takes without reciprocation.

Example:

You always drop everything to support a friend in crisis, but when you need help or support, they are mysteriously unavailable.

Detrimental Impact:

This imbalance leads to burnout, resentment, and emotional depletion. You may feel invisible, unappreciated, or used. Over time, it reinforces the belief that your needs are secondary.

8. The Silent Treatment/Stonewalling

Definition: Withdrawing from communication or refusing to engage—often used to punish, manipulate, or control.

Example:

After a disagreement, your partner gives you the silent treatment for days, refusing to speak to you or acknowledge your presence.

Detrimental Impact:

Silence is used as a weapon. It creates anxiety, emotional abandonment, and confusion. You may find yourself over-apologizing just to restore peace.

9. **Isolation**

Definition: Cutting someone off from friends, family, or support systems to increase dependence and control.

Example:

Your partner discourages you from seeing your friends, saying, "They're a bad influence. You don't need anyone but me."

Detrimental Impact:

Isolation weakens your support network and makes you more vulnerable to manipulation. You may feel lonely, trapped, or disconnected from your identity.

10. **Excessive Jealousy and Control**

Definition: Monitoring your whereabouts, demanding constant updates, or questioning your loyalty.

Example:

A partner insists on checking your phone or accuses you of cheating when you go out with friends.

Detrimental Impact:

This behavior creates fear, pressure, and emotional suffocation. You may feel like you are constantly defending yourself or walking on eggshells.

11. **Lack of Goodwill**

Definition: A consistent absence of kindness, empathy, or effort. The relationship feels cold, transactional, or indifferent.

Example:

When you share good news about a promotion, a friend responds, "Let's see how long that lasts," instead of celebrating with you.

Detrimental Impact:

Without goodwill, relationships become draining and emotionally barren. You may feel unseen, unsupported, or undervalued.

12. **Jealousy and Competition**

Definition: Constant comparison, feeling threatened by another's success, or trying to "outdo" them instead of supporting them.

Example:

You share your excitement about a new job, and your cousin immediately replies, "That's nothing, I had a better offer last year."

Detrimental Impact:

This creates tension, insecurity, and emotional distance. Instead of feeling uplifted, you feel diminished or dismissed.

Emotional and Psychological Impacts of Toxic Relationships

Toxic relationships don't just create conflict; they quietly reshape how you feel, think, and show up in the world. Long before you recognize the patterns, your mind and emotions often carry the weight of the harm. The following emotional and psychological impacts are real, and acknowledging them is the first step toward healing and reclaiming your sense of self.

- **Persistent Unhappiness:** The relationship feels heavy, tense, and draining—more conflict than connection.

- **Lack of Support:** You feel belittled, sabotaged, or dismissed instead of uplifted.

- **Emotional Exhaustion:** You're constantly "on edge," trying to avoid conflict or criticism.

- **Walking on Eggshells:** You monitor your words and actions to prevent triggering someone else's anger or withdrawal.

The impacts of toxic relationships are also physiological. It can cause chronic stress, affecting sleep, concentration, and even immune function. Your body knows when something isn't safe.

Repeated toxic encounters chip away at your confidence, clarity, and sense of self. By naming destructive relationship dynamics, you begin to take back your power and take steps toward building the healthy, reciprocal connections you deserve.

Self-Reflection Questions

1. Which toxic relationship patterns have you experienced?

2. Which patterns do you exhibit?

Generational Toxic Behaviors

Some toxic behaviors don't begin with us; they begin *before* us. They are passed down quietly, almost invisibly, through family norms, unspoken rules, and survival strategies that may once have protected earlier generations but now cause harm. When a toxic pattern appears across multiple generations, it's easy to mistake it for "just how our family is." However, generational behaviors, especially toxic ones, can be identified, understood, and broken with intention.

In Chapter 3: Am I a Doormat, I shared how I unknowingly followed in my mother's footsteps. I created a home that was orderly, structured, and disciplined, but lacked warmth, emotional safety, and nurturing connection. I believed love was something you demonstrated through responsibility and performance, not through affection or emotional presence. I didn't recognize this as a generational pattern. I simply thought it was the "right" way to parent.

Although I didn't change this pattern until my children were young adults, choosing to become a warm, emotionally available mother and grandmother has transformed our relationships. Still, the residual effects of that earlier parenting style linger. Generational wounds don't disappear overnight, but awareness opens the door to healing for us and for those who come after us.

What Makes Toxic Behaviors Generational

Toxic behaviors become generational when:

- It is repeated across multiple family members or generations.

- It is treated as normal, expected, or "just the way things are."

- It is rarely questioned or challenged.

- It is reinforced through family stories, roles, or expectations.

These patterns often begin as coping mechanisms. A grandmother who learned to stay silent to keep the peace may raise a daughter who believes her voice is dangerous. That daughter may then raise a child who apologizes for existing. The original wound gets passed down, even if the circumstances that created it are long gone.

Common Examples of Generational Toxic Behaviors

- **Avoiding conflict at all costs:** Families that equate disagreement with disrespect often raise children who fear speaking up or setting boundaries.

- **Emotional suppression:** Families that never talk about feelings often produce adults who don't know how to identify or express their own emotions.

- **Rigid gender roles or expectations:** "Good women do..." or "Real men don't..." can shape identity in limiting and harmful ways.

- **Normalizing disrespect or control:** If yelling, manipulation, or silent treatment were common in the home, they can feel familiar—even when they're unhealthy.

Self-Reflection Questions to Identify Generational Toxic Patterns

Recognizing generational toxicity requires curiosity, honesty, and compassion. These questions may help uncover family patterns.

- What behaviors did I learn growing up that I now struggle with in my adult relationships?

- Which toxic patterns do my parents, grandparents, siblings, or extended family exhibit?

- What did my family teach me, directly or indirectly, about conflict, love, boundaries, and self-worth?

- Are there behaviors I've always accepted as "normal" that actually cause me pain?

- Do I react in ways that feel automatic, even when I know they don't serve me?

Pay attention to emotional reactions that feel bigger than the moment. Those often point to inherited wounds rather than present-day realities.

Why Identifying Generational Toxic Patterns Matters

When you name a generational pattern, you interrupt its power. You stop blaming yourself for behaviors you didn't choose, and you begin choosing new ones. You become the generation that says, *"This ends with me."* That choice is not only healing for you; it becomes a gift to everyone who comes after you.

Breaking generational toxicity is an act of courage, clarity, and self-respect. It is the moment you stop repeating what hurt you and start creating what heals you.

When Awareness Becomes Power

Identifying these toxic relationship patterns is not about villainizing others. It's about honoring yourself. Once you see the signs, you can't unsee them. This clarity is a radical act of self-respect.

In Action #3, we'll explore how to respond to these patterns with boundaries, courage, and compassion. But for now, take a breath. Naming the pattern is the first act of power. You're already in motion.

Chapter Six

Action #2: Seek Clarity and Support

Let's begin with a vivid image:

Picture yourself in a smoke-filled room. Smoke appears out of nowhere and quickly fills the space. It clouds your vision, chokes your breath, and disorients your sense of direction. You can't see the exits. You can't even trust your instincts.

Toxic relationship patterns—whether with a partner, colleague, friend, or family member—are like that smoke. They descend without warning, distort your reality, and leave you questioning your own judgment. You may give the person the benefit of the doubt. You may even blame yourself:

"I'm overreacting."

"I must have caused this."

"Maybe I deserved it."

But then it happens again. And again.

Action #2: Seek Clarity and Support provides two essential lifelines:

- ways to help you recognize and name what you're truly experiencing—emotionally and mentally.

- support and resources to help you navigate this journey without feeling alone.

Clarity grounds you; support strengthens you. Together, they become your compass when the smoke of toxicity tries to sweep you away.

Toxic relationships scramble your emotional signals. One moment you feel anger, the next guilt, then shame, sadness, or numbness. Sometimes there are even glimmers of hope when things feel good again. Without clarity, these shifting emotions can trap you in a cycle of confusion and self-doubt.

Part of what makes clarity so difficult is the emotional whiplash these relationships create—moments of warmth mixed with moments of harm. Your mind becomes preoccupied with managing the next emotional shift, rather than seeing the bigger picture. This inconsistency keeps you off balance. You're reacting, not reflecting.

Yet seeking clarity is one of the most powerful acts of self-respect you can offer yourself. It isn't about judging the other person; it's about honoring your own emotional reality. It's choosing to tell yourself the truth, even when that truth is uncomfortable.

Clarity rarely arrives with fanfare. It's quiet. It's steady. It's the inner knowing that whispers, "This isn't right," or "Something needs to change." Even when the truth stings, clarity brings relief. It settles your spirit.

Another barrier to clarity is the tension of holding two truths at once: "I care about this person" and "This behavior is harming me." That conflict—known as cognitive dissonance—creates mental fog. Seeking clarity helps dissolve that fog by allowing you to face the truth with compassion rather than denial.

And remember: clarity doesn't require immediate action. You don't have to make a big decision today. Clarity simply asks you to see things as they are. Action comes later. For now, clarity is enough.

How to Seek Clarity

1. **Pause and Name Your Feelings**

   Instead of pushing through a toxic interaction on autopilot, pause to identify what you are feeling. Ask yourself: *What am I feeling right now—anger, anxiety, sadness, resentment, fear?* Naming your emotions is like turning on the lights in a dark room. It helps you see yourself more clearly.

   In addition, use this simple grounding exercise to help you pause and reflect.

   Place your hand on your chest and take one slow breath. Ask yourself:

   "What is true right now?"

   Not what you hope.

   Not what you fear.

   Just what is true.

This simple exercise cuts through the emotional fog and brings you back to yourself.

2. **Journal Your Toxic Interactions**

Keep a record of interactions that leave you unsettled. Write down what happened, how it made you feel, and how you responded. Over time, this journal becomes a mirror—reflecting patterns, emotional truths, and areas where you may need to shift your response.

3. **Separate Patterns from Isolated Incidents**

Everyone makes mistakes. But repeated behavior is a pattern. Ask yourself: *Is this happening again and again, or was it a one-time mistake?* Clarity grows when you distinguish between isolated incidents and recurring harm.

4. **Listen to Your Body**

Toxic stress often shows up physically: headaches, tension, fatigue, and insomnia. Your body may register danger before your mind does. Pay attention to how you feel before, during, and after interactions. Your body is often the most honest narrator.

5. **Challenge the Self-Doubt**

Toxic dynamics plant seeds of confusion: *"Maybe I'm too sensitive." "I should just let it go."* Counter these thoughts with reality checks: *"Would I accept this behavior if it happened to someone I love?"*

Clarity means trusting your inner truth—even when others try to distort it. And with each moment of truth comes a deeper level of honesty—first with yourself, then with everyone else.

SEEKING SUPPORT

Clarity is powerful, but it's not meant to be carried alone. Support helps you stay anchored when the emotional terrain gets rough.

Toxic relationships often isolate you—emotionally, mentally, and sometimes physically. They make you doubt your perceptions, silence your voice, and shrink your needs. That's why support is not just helpful; it's essential. It reconnects you to truth, steadiness, and community.

Support also interrupts the secrecy that toxic dynamics depend on. When you speak your experience out loud to someone safe, the fog begins to lift. You hear yourself clearly. You feel less alone. You remember that your feelings matter.

Still, seeking support can feel vulnerable. You may worry about being judged, dismissed, or misunderstood. You may feel embarrassed for "letting it go on this long." You may fear that others won't believe you. These fears are common and part of what makes support so healing. It gives you a place where your truth can land softly.

How to Seek Support

1. **Confide in a Trusted Person**

   Identify and share your experiences with someone who listens without judgment. Choose someone who validates your feelings—not someone who dismisses or deflects them. Healthy support feels steady, calm, and respectful. You should leave the conversation feeling lighter, not more confused.

2. **Professional Guidance**

   Therapy is not a sign of weakness; it's a strategy for reclaiming your power. A counselor, therapist, or coach can help you process emotions, strengthen boundaries, and reframe distorted thinking. They offer tools you may not have learned growing up—especially if you were taught to minimize your needs or keep the peace at all costs.

3. **Support Groups**

   Whether in person or online, support groups offer connection and validation. Hearing others' stories can help you feel seen and remind you that you're not alone. Shared experiences break the illusion that you're the only one struggling or "should have known better."

4. **Workplace Resources**

   If the toxic relationship is at work, explore your Human Resources department, your Employee Assistance Program (EAP), if available, mediation, or professional networks. Confidential support can help you navigate workplace dynamics with clarity and confidence. Burnout, bullying, and chronic disrespect are not "just part of the job"—and you deserve support in addressing them.

5. **Spiritual or Faith-Based Support**
   Prayer, meditation, or connection with a spiritual leader can offer grounding and perspective. These practices remind you of your inherent worth, especially when others try to diminish it. Spiritual support can help you reconnect with your identity, your values, and your sense of purpose.

6. **Emergency Plans**
   If your safety is at risk, have a plan in place. Know where to turn: crisis hotlines, domestic violence shelters, and law enforcement. Preparation replaces paralysis with

empowerment. You are not meant to navigate danger alone.

Self-Reflection Questions

Clarity:

How do you currently seek clarity after a toxic relationship incident?

Support:

Which of the support resources are you most likely to seek?

Bringing Truth to Light

Toxic relationships thrive in secrecy and confusion. But when you bring them into the light, their grip weakens. Clarity helps you see the truth. Support enables you to carry it.

Seeking clarity and support doesn't mean you must cut ties immediately or take drastic action overnight. It means you're choosing to acknowledge and accept your reality. To stop gaslighting yourself. To prevent shrinking to fit someone else's comfort. To remember that you deserve care, respect, and safety.

Seeking clarity and support is not a luxury; it's a critical part of your healing. Use the tools in this chapter to begin releasing your doormat behaviors.

Chapter Seven

Action #3: Implement Boundaries and Consequences with Clarity and Confidence

In Chapter 3, *Am I a Doormat?*, you were invited to reflect on your own relationship patterns. If you've determined that you often say "yes" when you mean "no," prioritize others' needs over your own, or struggle to shut down disrespectful behavior, this chapter will help you implement boundaries and consequences with clarity and confidence. Let's first begin with an understanding of each.

BOUNDARIES: YOUR PERSONAL STANDARDS

Boundaries are the limits you set to protect your emotional, mental, and physical well-being. They define what's acceptable and unacceptable in your relationships—whether at home, at work, or in your social circles.

A boundary might sound like:

- "No, I can't volunteer this Sunday. I've set that time aside for my family."

- "I will no longer tolerate being yelled at during disagreements."

Boundaries aren't punishments. They're declarations of self-respect.

CONSEQUENCES: FOLLOWING THROUGH WITHOUT APOLOGY

Consequences are the actions you take when someone crosses a boundary. They are not about revenge or control—they're about accountability and self-protection.

For example:

- "I will not tolerate being yelled at. I'm taking a break now. We'll talk later when you're calm."

- If the behavior continues: "I'm stepping away now." Then walk away—no further explanation needed.

Consistency is key. Boundaries without consequences are suggestions. Consequences without consistency lose their power.

Strategies for Implementing Boundaries and Consequences

There came a point in my transformational healing when I realized something essential: if I didn't define the standards for how I was to be treated, other people would define them for me. So, I began identifying what respect looked like for me—not in wishful thinking, but in real, everyday interactions. And once I set those standards, I had to learn how to protect them. That meant implementing consequences when those standards were crossed, even when doing so felt uncomfortable or unfamiliar.

The eight strategies for implementing boundaries and consequences in this Chapter became the framework that helped me reshape my relationships with family, friends, and colleagues. This chapter isn't theory; it's my testimony. These strategies helped me speak up, step back, and stand firm.

And I'll be honest: I fumbled. A lot. There were moments when I set a boundary too softly or too late. Times when I enforced a consequence inconsistently. Times when guilt made me second-guess myself. Times when old habits tried to pull me back into silence or over-functioning. But each misstep taught me something. Each stumble strengthened my clarity. Each imperfect attempt was still progress.

These strategies are not one-size-fits-all. You'll need to adapt them to your personality, your values, and your circumstances. What matters most is that you begin. Boundary-setting is a skill, and like any skill, it grows with practice, patience, and self-compassion.

If this is new territory for you, I encourage you to explore additional books and resources on boundary-setting. Surround yourself with wisdom, tools, and voices that reinforce your growth. You deserve relationships that honor your worth—and boundaries are the path that leads you there.

Strategy #1: Be Honest and Authentic

Showing up as your authentic self—without pretense or fear—creates the foundation for genuine, respectful relationships. Honesty and authenticity align your words, values, and actions, fostering trust and emotional safety. When you communicate your needs, desires, and limits clearly, you invite others to do the same. This mutual transparency reduces confusion, resentment, and emotional strain.

Example:

After stepping into a new management role, your director often vents about leadership. Though you empathize, their negativity drains you and clouds your morale.

You choose to speak up with honesty and authenticity:

"These conversations are affecting my focus. I'd prefer to only discuss leadership when it directly impacts my role."

By setting this boundary, you preserve your energy and model respectful communication.

Strategy #2: Be Assertive, Not Passive-Aggressive

Assertiveness allows you to express your thoughts, feelings, and boundaries clearly and respectfully—without diminishing others. Passive-aggressive behavior masks discomfort through sarcasm, withdrawal, or indirect resistance. Assertiveness brings clarity and emotional honesty to your relationships.

I didn't learn assertiveness in my early years. I put in the work to cultivate this skill. I've learned to speak up without guilt and stand firm without hostility.

If assertiveness feels hard, start small: say "no" to minor requests, express preferences, or ask for what you need. Confidence grows with practice.

Example:

During a collaborative project, a colleague repeatedly misses deadlines, causing delays and increasing your workload.

You decide to be assertive and direct:

"The repeated missed deadlines are causing delays and affecting our timeline. Can we agree on clearer communication and a shared deadline schedule?"

The conversation is uncomfortable but productive. Your colleague adjusts, and your stress eases.

Strategy #3: Check Your Own Toxic Behavior

Before setting boundaries with others, examine your own patterns. Self-awareness is the foundation of healthy relationships. It requires courage, humility, and a willingness to grow.

Revisit the 12 toxic patterns in Chapter 4. Ask:

- Do I exhibit any of these behaviors?

- Have I contributed to the dysfunction?

If the answer is yes, don't blame—transform.

My Personal Example:

A few years into my second marriage, my spouse and I found ourselves in a cycle of toxic exchanges. Arguments often ended with him saying something cruel. At first, I blamed him entirely.

After deep self-reflection and prayer, I realized that my own communication had become condescending. I was speaking from a place of superiority, creating a power imbalance that left my spouse feeling belittled, unheard, and disrespected. His harshness was a defense shield against the imbalance I had unknowingly created.

To shift this dynamic, I changed my approach:

- I listened without interrupting.

- I used affirming language.

- I asked questions to understand, not to challenge him.

As I changed, so did he. The toxic cycle broke not because I demanded it, but because I removed the fuel that was feeding it.

The boundary I set was on myself. I chose to communicate differently. I decided to lead with respect.

Strategy #4: Make "No" a Part of Your Vocabulary

For people-pleasers, saying "no" feels unnatural. But learning to say "no" with grace and clarity is one of the most liberating skills you can develop. It's a verbal boundary that protects your time, energy, and peace.

Here's how I decide when and how to say no:

1. **I check in with my heart.** I ask myself how I *truly* feel about the request. For example, a friend invited me to a Paint & Sip. I learned that I don't enjoy this type of event, so I said no. We decided to go to a music event instead.

2. **I assess my capacity.** Being dependable matters to me, so I look at my schedule and workload to ensure I can follow through. If I'm stretched too thin, I honor that.

3. **I give myself time.** When I'm unsure, I don't rush into a yes. I say, "Let me think about it and get back to you." This gives me space to respond with intention.

4. **I keep it simple.** I don't overexplain or apologize for my no. In the Paint & Sip example, I simply said, "No, I don't enjoy those events."

5. **I address boundary violations directly.** If someone expects me to drop everything for an impromptu meeting, I respond with, "No, I'm not available right now. Let's find a time that works for both of us." This reinforces mutual respect.

Saying "no" is not rejection—it's protection. It's how we honor our needs and teach others to do the same.

Start with one "no" at a time. And if you slip and say yes when you meant no, give yourself grace. You're learning. You're growing. And every boundary you set is a step toward clarity and self-respect.

Strategy #5: Release the Illusion of Perfection in a Relationship

Reflecting on my own journey, I've had moments when I could have been more patient, loving, or thoughtful. Times when I said things I regretted or missed opportunities to resolve conflicts with grace. These experiences taught me a powerful truth: perfection is not the goal in relationships—authentic connection is.

I no longer expect flawlessness from myself or others. Instead, I choose relationships where we can show up fully—messy, growing, and real. I want the people in my life to feel safe being themselves, without having to perform or pretend. And I want that same freedom for myself: to be loved not for perfection, but for presence.

Healthy relationships prioritize growth over perfection. Mistakes will happen. But when there's a shared commitment to repair, understand, and respect one another, those imperfections become opportunities for deeper connection.

Signs that a relationship is rooted in value—not perfection:

- You genuinely enjoy each other's company.

- You both feel free to be yourselves.

- Mistakes are addressed collaboratively, not weaponized.

- There's a consistent effort to learn and grow together.

- You feel seen, heard, and supported—not judged.

Strategy #6: Consistently Enforce Boundaries with Consequences

Releasing "doormat" behavior begins with a mindset shift: recognizing your agency in how others treat you. For me, realizing I could teach people how to treat me through clear boundaries and consistent follow-through was a game-changer. It moved me from silent frustration to empowered self-respect.

When someone values you, they'll adjust once you communicate a boundary. But even well-meaning people can't honor boundaries they don't know exist. That's why direct, respectful communication is essential.

Still, some relationships require more than words. When boundaries are repeatedly crossed, consequences become necessary—not as punishment, but as accountability.

Yes, it takes effort. Yes, it requires patience. But the reward is worth it: healthier relationships and peace of mind.

Three ways I implement consequences for repeated toxic behavior:

1. **Assume ignorance before malice and act accordingly.**

   Not every boundary violation is intentional. Some people need time to unlearn harmful habits.

   Example: A friend regularly arrives 30+ minutes late to leave for events together. Instead of assuming disrespect, you recognize poor time management. You communicate that you'll wait only 15 minutes. When they arrive late, you've already left. After a few missed meetups, they begin showing up on time.

2. **Shift the dynamic of a toxic interaction.**

If something feels disrespectful, trust your gut. In Chapter 5, I outlined five steps to gain clarity:

- pause and name your feelings

- journal the interactions

- separate patterns from isolated incidents

- listen to your body

- challenge self-doubt

Once you've gained clarity, change how you engage.

Example: Two verbal presentations to your manager end in harsh criticism with no constructive feedback. You switch to submitting draft presentations via email and request written feedback. This protects your emotional well-being and invites more balanced, actionable input.

3. **Be brief, respectful, and consistent.**

When a boundary is crossed, respond calmly and immediately. Keep it short. Follow through with the consequences. Repeat as needed.

Example: Your partner frequently interrupts you during disagreements. You say, "It's important that both our voices are heard. Let's continue when you're ready to hear me out." Then you walk away. This respectful disengagement reinforces your boundary without escalating the conflict.

If someone repeatedly disrespects your boundaries and shows no willingness to change, it may be time to reevaluate the relationship. Chapter 8 offers guidance on navigating that difficult decision with clarity and compassion.

Strategy #7: Don't Let Others Steal Your Joy

Joy is not a fleeting emotion. It's a deep, internal state anchored in your self-worth, peace, and purpose. It's the light within you that no one else can manufacture or extinguish. Yet, toxic interactions can pull you into someone else's storm of unhappiness, anger, or bitterness.

Releasing doormat behavior means learning to protect your joy, especially after challenging encounters.

Three ways I reclaim my joy after toxic interactions:

1. **Communicate, follow-through, and release.**

   Once you've clearly stated your boundary and implemented a consequence, your work is done. Let go of the emotional residue and return to your grounded self.

2. **Don't internalize other people's chaos.**

Someone else's dysfunction is not your assignment. Their anger, insecurity, or bitterness often has little to do with you. You are responsible for your own emotional health—not for fixing theirs. Refuse to absorb what isn't yours.

3. **Return to your peaceful space.**

When toxicity threatens your balance, retreat to what restores you—a walk, music, prayer, or quiet reflection. Peace is your reset button. Joy is waiting on the other side.

Protecting your joy is not selfish—it's sacred. You are allowed to be happy even when others aren't. Reclaiming your joy after toxic encounters is a radical act of self-respect. It reminds you—and the world—that your spirit is not up for grabs.

Strategy #8: Have the Courage to Let Go When Boundaries Are Continually Crossed

Establishing boundaries is powerful. Communicating them is brave. Consistently enforcing them is transformative. But what if none of that leads to change?

When boundaries are repeatedly violated and consequences ignored, it's time to ask: Can this relationship continue in its current form?

We'll explore this more in Chapter 8. For now, here are a few truths about letting go:

- Letting go doesn't always mean cutting someone off. In some cases—like a toxic manager or a difficult family member, elimination isn't possible. But emotional detachment is.

- Letting go means you stop pouring energy into a dynamic that refuses to honor your boundaries. You stop chasing change in someone who won't choose it.

- Letting go means grieving the relationship you hoped for and accepting the one that exists. From this place of clarity, you can decide how to interact in a way that protects your peace.

Letting go takes courage. But staying in emotional captivity—waiting for someone else to change—is harder. Choosing peace over chaos isn't weakness. It's wisdom. And it's the next brave step in reclaiming your life.

Boundaries and Consequences Self-Reflection Activity

Think of a relationship where you'd like to establish boundaries and consequences. Craft a boundary and consequence that fits your personality, values, and circumstances.

Putting Boundaries into Daily Practice

Implementing boundaries and consequences can feel uncomfortable at first. You may face resistance from others and even from within yourself. But stay the course. Be consistent. Be kind to yourself.

I can tell you from experience: the payoff is profound. Peace. Confidence. Joy. And the quiet strength of knowing that I am walking in my authentic self.

Chapter Eight

Action #4: Know Yourself and Grow Yourself

At age 40, I made one of the hardest decisions of my life: I ended my 18-year marriage. It wasn't a sudden choice. It was the result of years spent tangled in toxic patterns I didn't know how to resolve.

Later, with healing and reflection, I understood how my own toxic and doormat behaviors played a role in our toxic relationship patterns. I wasn't just grieving the loss of a marriage. I was grieving the loss of myself.

I walked away carrying the weight of fractured relationships, not just with my spouse, but with my family, and most painfully, with myself. I was emotionally depleted, bitter, and unequipped with the skills to change relationship dynamics.

But somewhere in my brokenness, I had the resilience to begin a profound journey of personal, professional, and spiritual growth. I didn't just want to heal—I wanted to evolve. And so I did.

Growth Releases Doormat Behaviors

Growth and releasing doormat behaviors go hand in hand. It requires a courageous journey inward to align your actions with your values, your voice, and your worth.

Four areas of growth became my foundation for transformation:

1. Self-awareness

2. Self-esteem

3. Assertiveness

4. Conflict resolution

Each of these areas is rich with research and wisdom. I encourage you to explore them deeply. But for now, let me share how I grew in these areas, and how you can too.

Are you ready to do the inner work to grow in areas to help you release doormat behaviors? Let's walk this path together.

SELF-AWARENESS: THE FIRST STEP TOWARD WHOLENESS

Self-awareness is the ability to see yourself clearly—your thoughts, emotions, patterns, values, and impact you have on others. It is the heartbeat of emotional maturity, relational integrity, and personal power.

And here's the truth: self-awareness isn't automatic. It doesn't come with age or experience.

I've met young adults with remarkable insight and older adults who've never paused to reflect. Often, we don't realize we lack it until someone lovingly points it out, or until life forces us to look inward.

My desire to grow my self-awareness came from a longing to live in alignment with my values. But first, I had to name those values. I had to recognize when I was acting against them.

Here's how my lack of self-awareness showed up in my relationships.

- I didn't realize how my own behaviors were fueling toxic interactions.

- I couldn't regulate my emotions. I wore them on my sleeve, raw and unfiltered.

- I didn't know my limits or boundaries, so I let others cross them.

- I misread relationships, missing signs of disrespect or emotional neglect.

How I Grew My Self-Awareness

My growth didn't happen overnight. It was slow, sacred, and sometimes painful—like a caterpillar transforming into a butterfly. Each step was a turning point, a moment of clarity that deepened my understanding of who I am and how I show up in the world.

Here are the tools and strategies that helped me evolve into a more conscious, grounded, and empowered version of myself.

1. **Shifting from a Fixed to a Growth Mindset**

   My journey to self-awareness began with a shift in my mindset. To grow, I could no longer adopt the view that how I am is fixed and unchangeable. I had to believe that change was possible. That I wasn't stuck. That my past didn't define my future. Embracing a growth mindset meant seeing every experience as an opportunity to learn more about myself, seeing mistakes as lessons, and using feedback as fuel. It meant choosing curiosity over shame. With an open mind, heart, and spirit, I was now ready to know myself and grow myself.

2. Spending Time Alone: Getting to Know Me

I carved out time to be with myself—not just physically, but emotionally. I went to restaurants alone, took walks, danced, journaled, and sat in silence. I asked myself questions I had long avoided:

- What do I genuinely enjoy?

- What drains me?

- What beliefs have I inherited that no longer serve me?

- What do I value most?

This solitude became sacred. In the quiet, I could finally hear my own voice.

3. **Immersing Myself in Self-Development Literature**

Books became my lifeline. I devoured titles on emotional intelligence, communication, healing, relationships, and growth. Each page offered new language for my experiences and new frameworks for understanding myself. I didn't just read—I applied it. I highlighted, annotated, and revisited chapters that spoke to my soul. These books helped me name patterns, reframe pain, and envision new possibilities.

4. **Exploring Personality and Strengths Assessments**

Tools like Myers-Briggs, CliftonStrengths, DISC, and EQ helped me understand my natural tendencies and blind spots. They gave me words for my strengths and helped me appreciate others' differences.

5. **Practicing Introspection and Reflection**

After every interaction, especially the hard ones, I paused.

- What was I feeling?

- What triggered me?

- What did I learn about myself?

This practice helped me uncover unconscious habits and emotional blind spots. Over time, I became less reactive and more intentional.

6. **Choosing Mindfulness vs. Autopilot**

When my daughter was little, she'd chatter away while I cooked, cleaned, and mentally replayed my day. One afternoon, she asked me what she had just said. I couldn't answer. I had been physically present but emotionally absent and operating in autopilot.

Autopilot may feel efficient, but it quietly disconnects you from your own life. You stop noticing your emotions, your body's signals, and the people right in front of you. It becomes easier to tolerate disrespect, overlook red flags, and repeat old patterns because you're not fully aware of what's happening in the moment. Over time, autopilot can numb your joy, weaken your relationships, and keep you stuck in cycles you never consciously chose.

Years later, I began practicing mindfulness—being fully present with my thoughts, feelings, and surroundings. It helped me savor joy, manage conflict, and respond with intention rather than impulse. During challenging encounters, practicing mindfulness allowed me to assess what was happening inside me, name what I was feeling, and pause to decide how to respond.

7. Welcoming Feedback as a Gift

Feedback used to feel like criticism. But I learned to see it as a mirror—one that could reflect both my strengths and my growth edges.

I invited input from my spouse, mentors, colleagues, and friends. We played "Tabletopics" games to spark honest conversations. This was a great way to learn how people see me. I also stopped getting defensive during tough feedback conversations so that I could absorb and be open to what was being said.

Feedback helped me see how my actions aligned or misaligned with my values.

The Freedom that Comes with Self-Awareness

Self-awareness isn't a destination—it's a lifelong practice. These tools didn't just help me understand myself; they helped me honor myself.

They gave me:

- The courage to change.

- The clarity to choose.

- The compassion to grow.

When you know who you are deeply and unapologetically, you stop needing others to validate you. You stop shrinking to fit someone else's comfort.

You stand in your truth. You speak with your full voice. You live with integrity.

And that, dear reader, is where healing begins.

SELF-ESTEEM: RECLAIMING THE WORTH WITHIN

Self-esteem is the internal belief that you are worthy of love, respect, and dignity—not because of what you do, but because of who you are. It's the quiet confidence that lets you stand in your truth without shrinking, apologizing, or performing.

Healthy self-esteem isn't arrogance, perfection, or pretending to be strong. It's the steady knowing that your voice, your needs, and your presence matter.

Without self-esteem, breaking free from doormat behaviors becomes almost impossible. When you don't believe in your own worth, you tolerate mistreatment because you think you deserve it. You silence yourself to keep the peace. You overextend yourself to earn approval. You accept crumbs because you don't believe you're worthy of the whole table.

Releasing doormat behaviors requires more than courage. It requires a renewed understanding of your God-given value.

That's why rebuilding self-esteem is foundational. You cannot set boundaries if you don't believe you're worth protecting. It is the soil where confidence grows, where boundaries take root, and where self-respect becomes non-negotiable.

What Low Self-Esteem Looked Like for Me

Growing up as a Black girl in the 60s and 70s shaped the internal messages I carried. I absorbed the belief that I had to work twice as hard to be seen, respected, or considered worthy. I learned early that my skin tone, my features, my voice, and even my emotions were judged through a harsher lens. I didn't realize how deeply those messages had settled into my spirit. They whispered that I wasn't enough. They taught me to question my beauty, shrink my presence, and doubt my worth.

At home, my parents worked hard and provided a comfortable, middle-class life. But behind closed doors, I felt the pressure to be well-spoken, neat, and carry myself just right—as if my value depended on flawless presentation.

The world told me I wasn't enough, and home told me I had to be perfect. Those mixed messages wrapped themselves around my identity before I even knew how to define myself.

So, I became an expert at camouflaging my low self-esteem. I hid behind external markers of confidence—looking put together, communicating clearly, showing up strong, and pretending I had everything under control. People saw the polished version of me, the woman who seemed steady and capable. But inside, I was fighting a quieter battle: learning how to love myself as a Black woman in a world that had fed me negative messages about my beauty, my value, and my place.

I had internalized so many of those lies that they shaped the way I saw myself long before I ever found the courage to challenge them. The disconnect between who I appeared to be and who I felt like on the inside created a loneliness I didn't know how to name.

But the military became a turning point. It challenged me, stretched me, and gave me opportunities to rise. I mastered my roles, overcame obstacles, and stepped into leadership. For the first time, I began to take pride in my abilities. I felt strong. Capable. Resilient. I started to build a healthy respect for myself.

Marriage and motherhood added to that sense of accomplishment. But even with those external milestones, something was still missing. I hadn't yet learned how to love myself from the inside out. And when my marriage ended, my self-esteem plummeted. That's when the real work began—not just to rebuild, but to rediscover the woman I was always meant to be.

How I Elevated My Self-Esteem

Before I could elevate my self-esteem, I had to first acknowledge that it wasn't something that would magically rise on its own. It required intention. It required honesty. And it required me to show up for myself in ways I never had before.

Little by little, I began rebuilding the parts of me that had been overlooked, silenced, or dismissed. I didn't transform overnight. I grew through consistent choices—choices that honored my body, my voice, my gifts, my goals, and my God-given worth.

These are the practices that helped me rise into a healthier, stronger, more grounded version of myself.

1. **Practiced Meaningful Self-Care**

While moving through the healing process, I paid more attention to self-care. I also curated a style that better reflected my personality and made me feel beautiful. I took up running—not to lose weight—but to feel strong and clear-headed. I nourished my body with healthy food and movement. Feeling vibrant in my own skin helped me reconnect with my worth.

2. **Started Loving Me for Me**

I embraced daily affirmations and replaced negative self-talk with words of kindness. I stopped comparing myself to others and began celebrating my uniqueness. I created my own style, honored my attributes, and gave myself permission to be fully me—flaws and all.

3. **Invested in Personal and Professional Growth**

I joined Toastmasters and delivered ten speeches, which improved my communication skills and confidence. I was later elected President of our chapter and served for two years. I attended workshops, pursued training, and committed to excellence in my career.

Researching, creating, and facilitating leadership and professional development courses for over fifteen years has also expanded my personal and professional growth. Every skill I sharpened reminded me that I was capable and worthy.

4. Set and Achieved Meaningful Goals

I began setting goals that aligned with my values, and that helped me grow into who I wanted to become. Whether it was completing a course, organizing an event, creating and facilitating classes, or writing, each goal became a stepping stone toward self-belief.

5. Built a Supportive and Nurturing Network

I surrounded myself with friends who uplifted me, challenged me, and reminded me of my value. These relationships became mirrors—

reflecting back the strength and beauty I couldn't always see in myself. We celebrated each other's wins and held space for each other's struggles.

6. Volunteered to Serve Others in My Church

Serving in my faith community gave me purpose and connection. Whether I was teaching, organizing, or simply showing up, I felt seen and valued. Giving back reminded me that I had something to offer, and that my presence mattered.

Loving Yourself into a Stronger Self-Esteem

Elevating self-esteem isn't about perfection. It's about compassion. It's about learning to see yourself through the eyes of grace, not judgment. The more I honored my journey, the more I could stand tall in my truth. And the more I loved myself, the less I needed others to define me.

ASSERTIVENESS: FINDING YOUR VOICE WITHOUT APOLOGY

Assertiveness is the ability to express your feelings, needs, and boundaries in a way that is clear, direct, and respectful. It's not aggression. It's not passivity. It's the sweet spot where your voice matters and your dignity remains intact.

For years, I didn't know how to be assertive. I avoided conflict, said yes when I meant no, and allowed disrespect to go unchecked. I thought being "nice" meant being silent. But silence cost me my peace.

I remember a moment at work when a colleague repeatedly interrupted me during meetings. I used to shrink back, thinking it wasn't worth the confrontation. But one day, I calmly said, "I'd like to finish my thought before we move on." That simple sentence was a breakthrough. I had honored my voice, and it felt powerful.

How I Learned to Be Assertive

Becoming assertive was a slow, intentional process of replacing old habits—people-pleasing, shrinking myself, and remaining silent—with new ones. As I grew tired of carrying the weight of unspoken frustrations, I realized that honoring my voice was not selfish but necessary. Assertiveness became the practice that helped me speak with clarity, stand in my truth, and protect my peace. What follows is how I learned to step into that strength, one courageous choice at a time.

1. Strengthened My Skills

I didn't wake up one day to find myself magically assertive. I had to build that skill the same way you build any muscle—through learning, repetition, and stretching beyond my comfort zone.

I read books that taught me the language of assertiveness: "I feel...," "I need...," "I prefer...," and "That doesn't work for me." I attended workshops where I practiced speaking up in safe environments.

Joining Toastmasters was a turning point. Standing in front of a room, heart pounding, and still choosing to speak taught me that my voice could be steady even when my nerves weren't. Each speech strengthened my confidence. Each evaluation taught me how to communicate clearly and respectfully. Over time, I learned that assertiveness wasn't about being loud; it was about being grounded.

2. **Built My Self-Esteem and Confidence**

Assertiveness is impossible when you don't believe your voice matters.

As I worked on my self-esteem, I stopped chasing approval and started honoring my truth. I began to see myself as someone deserving of respect, not someone who had to earn it by over-giving or staying quiet.

I learned to separate my identity from other people's reactions. If someone didn't like my boundary, that didn't mean I was wrong. It simply meant they were used to the old version of me. The more I valued myself, the more natural it became to speak up. Assertiveness became an extension of self-respect, not a performance.

3. **Practiced Mindfulness**

Mindfulness helped me slow down enough to notice what I was feeling in that moment.

Before, I reacted automatically by saying yes when I meant no, laughing off disrespect, or swallowing my needs. But mindfulness taught me to pause, breathe, and check in with myself.

I started asking simple questions:

- What am I feeling right now?

- What do I need?

- What would honoring myself look like in this moment?

This awareness allowed me to respond instead of react. It helped me speak from a place of clarity rather than fear. Mindfulness became the bridge between my emotions and my voice.

Mindfulness helped me tune into my emotions and needs in real time. As a result, I began responding with intention and authenticity.

4. Started Small

I didn't begin by confronting the biggest issues. I started with the small ones—the everyday moments where I had been shrinking.

I practiced saying no to invitations I didn't want. I voiced my preferences instead of defaulting to what others wanted. I corrected people gently when they misrepresented my thoughts or needs.

These small acts were like training wheels. Each time I honored myself in a minor situation, I gained courage for the bigger ones. I learned that assertiveness didn't have to be dramatic; it could be simple, steady, and consistent.

5. **Practiced Assertiveness Regularly**

Assertiveness is not a one-time event; it's a lifestyle.

- I rehearsed conversations before having them.

- I reflected afterward on what went well and what I could improve.

- I reminded myself that growth is messy and that missteps were part of the process.

Over time, speaking up became less of a battle and more of a habit. I stopped over-explaining. I stopped apologizing for having needs. I stopped shrinking to make others comfortable. I kept showing up for myself, even when it felt awkward or unfamiliar.

And slowly, I became a woman who could stand in her truth without trembling.

Owning Your Voice Through Assertiveness

Assertiveness is a gift you give yourself. It's the moment you stop whispering your worth and begin living it out loud. It's the bridge between knowing who you are and honoring that truth in every room you enter.

When you speak with clarity and compassion, you set a new standard for how others may treat you, and you set a new standard for how you treat yourself. Each time you choose your voice over silence, you reinforce the truth that you are worthy of respect, worthy of boundaries, and worthy of being heard.

Assertiveness becomes more than a skill. It becomes an act of self-love, a declaration that you will no longer shrink to make others comfortable. It is the quiet, steady courage of someone who finally knows their value and refuses to abandon it.

CONFLICT RESOLUTION: HEALING THROUGH HEALTHY DIALOGUE

Conflict is inevitable. But how we handle it determines whether it becomes a catalyst for growth or a breeding ground for resentment. For those of us who've struggled with doormat behaviors, conflict can feel overwhelming and unsafe. We may turn to toxic relationship patterns such as passive-aggressiveness, stonewalling, or disappearing emotionally.

Healthy conflict, rooted in honesty, respect, and emotional integrity, is a doorway to deeper understanding and stronger relationships. Learning to resolve conflict with confidence is one of the most transformative steps in releasing doormat behaviors.

How I Grew in Conflict Resolution

Conflict used to terrify me. I saw it as a threat—something to avoid, tiptoe around, or silence myself to escape. But over time, I learned that conflict isn't the enemy. Avoidance is.

When handled with honesty and emotional maturity, conflict becomes a powerful teacher. It reveals truth, deepens connection, and strengthens our sense of self.

Here are five ways I stopped running from conflict and instead embraced it as a pathway to healing, clarity, and healthier relationships.

1. **Engaged with Trust and Respect**

   I entered conversations assuming positive intent. I reminded myself that most people aren't trying to hurt me; they're trying to be heard. This mindset softened my defensiveness and opened the door to mutual respect.

2. **Separated the Issue from the Person**

I learned to address the behavior or concern without attacking the individual. "I felt dismissed when my ideas weren't acknowledged" is very different from "You never listen." This shift helped me stay grounded and constructive.

3. **Practiced Active Listening**

I used eye contact, open body language, and verbal cues to show I was fully present. I listened not just to respond, but to understand.

4. **Asked Clarifying Questions and Paraphrased**

When something felt unclear, I asked, "Can you help me understand what you meant?" I repeated back what I heard to confirm understanding. This built trust and reduced miscommunication.

5. Sought Common Ground

Instead of trying to "win" the conflict, I looked for shared values and mutual goals. What do we both want? Where can we meet in the middle? This approach turned conflict into collaboration.

Conflict Resolution as a Path to Growth

Resolving conflict isn't about being right; it's about being real. It's choosing to show up with honesty instead of hiding, empathy instead of ego, and a willingness to grow instead of a need to win.

When you approach conflict with emotional maturity, you stop treating it like a threat and start recognizing it as a doorway. Every hard conversation becomes a chance to deepen understanding, strengthen connection, and honor your own voice.

Over time, conflict stops feeling like a battlefield and becomes a bridge—one that leads you toward healthier relationships, clearer boundaries, and a more grounded version of yourself.

And here's the truth that changes everything: when you stop running from conflict, you stop running from yourself.

PUTTING YOUR GROWTH JOURNEY INTO ACTION

Your journey of growth is yours alone. It doesn't have to include every area I've shared. Maybe you'll start with self-awareness. Perhaps you'll begin by being more assertive. Pause and ask yourself, "What do I need right now?"

Whatever path you choose, make it your own. Reflect on what resonates. Take one step at a time. Growth isn't about rushing. It's about becoming.

So, decide today how you want to move forward in knowing yourself and growing yourself. You are worthy of becoming the authentic, empowered version of yourself. The one who no longer shrinks, bends, or disappears, but rises, rooted in truth and radiant in purpose.

Know Yourself and Grow Yourself Self-Reflection Activity

Write down 2 – 3 personal growth activities you will begin this month.

Chapter Nine

Action #5: Determine How or If the Relationship Can Continue

You've named the toxic patterns, asserted your voice, set clear boundaries, and implemented consequences with no success. There may come a point when you must decide whether or how to continue a relationship.

This is a deeply personal decision. Depending on the nature of the relationship, it can be heart-wrenching. Your decision may ripple out to affect others—family, children, mutual friends, or colleagues.

How you decide to proceed cannot be made in haste or anger. It must be rooted in clarity, truth, self-respect, and a commitment to your physical and emotional safety.

This chapter cannot provide the answer for you. Instead, it offers a framework to help you assess the next steps through deep, thought-provoking questions. I ask that you approach each question with the honesty and courage it deserves. Are you ready?

Assess the Person's Willingness to Change

Questions to consider:

1. Has the person started taking responsibility for their toxic or disrespectful behavior?

2. Can the person admit when they are wrong in a specific situation?

3. Has the person taken noticeable steps to change?

4. Is the person doing better in respecting my boundaries?

5. Is the person defensive when I try to discuss or resolve the situation?

6. Is the person open to feedback on how their behavior is negatively affecting me?

Assess the Psychological and Emotional Toll on You

Questions to consider:

1. Do I feel emotionally safe expressing my thoughts and feelings?

2. Do I walk on eggshells around this person—bracing for conflict?

3. Am I constantly second-guessing myself or my decisions because of this relationship?

4. Has this relationship changed how I see myself—for better or worse?

5. Do I feel emotionally exhausted or uplifted after spending time with this person?

6. Do I feel more anxious, sad, or numb in the relationship?

Assess If the Relationship is Abusive

Questions to consider:

1. Do I feel afraid of my partner's reactions, even when I've done nothing wrong?

2. Does my partner insult, belittle, or humiliate me in private or public?

3. Am I isolated from friends, family, or support systems because of this relationship?

4. Does my partner use threats, guilt, manipulation, or gaslighting in the relationship?

5. Do I feel trapped, confused, or like I'm losing myself in the relationship?

Assess Your Non-Negotiables and Dealbreakers

Questions to consider:

1. What are my non-negotiables and dealbreakers?

2. Which of my non-negotiables or dealbreakers is this person violating?

3. Have I seen any improvements from this person in these areas?

Assess Seeking Therapy as a Next Step

Questions to consider:

Therapy for Myself

1. Can therapy help me identify and stop repeating "doormat" behaviors, such as people-pleasing or avoiding conflict?

2. Do I struggle to trust my own judgment or set boundaries?

3. Do I need help determining the next step in my relationship?

Therapy for Me and My Spouse or Partner

1. Are we both willing to participate in therapy and do the work?

2. Do we want to improve our relationship, or are we seeking validation or blame?

3. Are we both open to hearing brutal truths
    and making changes?

Therapy for a Troubled Parent-Child Relationship

1. Are there behavioral issues that seem
    rooted in deeper emotional needs?

2. Does the child express feeling
    misunderstood, unheard, or unsafe?

3. Are there co-parenting issues that are
    affecting the child?

Assess Alternative Relationship Options without Completely Letting Go

It is simply not possible to end or avoid all relationships. You have the power to determine how best to interact in each relationship. You have the power to decide if it is time to let it go altogether.

1. A romantic relationship may be better suited as a platonic friendship.

2. A relative relationship outside your home may shift to limited and surface-level contact.

3. A friendship may fade to an associate relationship with limited connection.

4. A colleague relationship may shift from a daily, personal connection to a limited, professional contact.

5. A manager relationship that you've determined does not have good intentions may change to documenting and protecting yourself.

6. A partner or spouse relationship may shift to peaceful coexistence without intimacy or separation.

Evaluate Your Answers and Options

Before moving forward, it's important to pause and reflect on what your answers reveal. This section invites you to step back and notice the patterns in your relationships—what's been consistent, what's shifted, and what choices lie ahead. By identifying these trends and exploring your options, you'll gain clarity and confidence to make decisions that align with your values, needs, and growth.

1. What relationship trends are you seeing in your responses?

2. What relationship options are you considering?

3. How can you engage professional support?

Communicate Your Decision

Whether you choose to continue, redefine, or end the relationship, clarity is essential. Communicate your decision with honesty and firmness.

- If you're continuing, clearly outline your expectations, boundaries, and what you need moving forward.

- If you're redefining the relationship, explain what that new dynamic will look like and what behaviors are no longer acceptable.

- If you choose to end the relationship, do so with dignity. You don't need to justify your decision to everyone, but you do owe yourself peace. Ending a relationship is not a failure. It's a courageous act of self-preservation and growth.

Honor Your Decision

You may experience grief, guilt, or doubt after making a decision regarding your relationship. That's normal. Choosing yourself is not selfish. It's sacred.

You are not alone in this process. Many people have stood at this same crossroads, unsure of what to do next. What matters most is that you honor your truth and protect your well-being. Relationships are meant to nourish, not diminish. You deserve a connection that uplifts, respects, and supports you.

Take your time. Breathe. Reflect. And when you're ready, choose the path that leads you closer to peace.

Chapter Ten

Action #6: Restoration and Healing: Say Goodbye to Doormat Behaviors

For years, I operated as a doormat, silencing myself to mistreatment, swallowing disrespect like bitter medicine, and engaging in toxic relationship patterns because I didn't know any better. The end of my 18-year marriage shattered me, but it also cracked open a door I had long ignored: the door to healing.

My restoration and healing journey was not a single moment. There were thousands of difficult, sometimes painful, small steps toward reclaiming my voice, my worth, and my peace.

I was not alone in my restoration and healing journey. Therapy, support groups, spiritual nourishment, and friends supported me along the way.

Eight Restoration and Healing Lifelines

This chapter isn't just a list of what I did; it's a living testimony of how God's grace and intentional choices pulled me out of the deepest parts of myself.

These eight restoration and healing lifelines became the scaffolding that held me together when everything else felt like it was falling apart. They didn't just help me recover, they helped me rise from brokenness to wholeness, one intentional act at a time.

1. **Restoration and Healing Through Loving Myself**

Loving myself didn't come naturally. I had to intentionally unlearn years of self-criticism and relearn how to see myself through a lens of compassion. I implemented daily affirmations —simple, but powerful. I'd look in the mirror and say, "You look good," even when I didn't feel it.

As my self-esteem grew, I embraced the beauty of my attributes—the curve of my smile, the strength in my legs, the sparkle in my eyes when I laughed. I started dressing in attire that made me feel alive. I wrote love letters to myself in my journal.

Loving myself continues to be a daily practice—one that reminds me, I am enough.

2. **Restoration and Healing Through Therapy**

Therapy wasn't just a tool. It saved my life. Not overnight, but over time. My therapist challenged my distorted beliefs, helped me unpack emotional wounds, and guided me to understand toxic patterns in myself and others.

My therapy also came in other forms. Self-development books became my companions. Faith-based guidance gave me language for my pain. Support groups gave me mirrors to see myself more clearly.

I also found healing in community. For almost a decade, I've led a women's life group where we cry, laugh, pray, and grow together. We share our stories without shame. We hold each other accountable. We remind each other that healing is not linear—and that we are never alone.

3. **Restoration and Healing Through Strengthening My Faith**

My faith is my anchor. When the storms of life threatened to drown me, it was prayer that kept me afloat. I'd sit in silence, tears streaming down my face, whispering scriptures like they were nourishment to my soul: "I am fearfully and wonderfully made." "God is close to the brokenhearted."

I found refuge in spiritual journaling, worship, and quiet walks where I'd talk to God as my friend. My faith didn't erase the pain; it gave it purpose. It reminded me that restoration is holy work. That healing is sacred. That I am held, even when I feel alone.

4. **Restoration and Healing Through Dedicated Health Practices**

My body carried the weight of my emotional pain. I had to learn how to let it go. I started running daily—not for fitness, but for space to meditate. I added yoga and deep breathing, line dancing, and an array of group exercise classes to my regimen.

I also became more mindful of healthy eating and made necessary dietary changes. I prioritized sleep and rest as if they were sacred.

5. **Restoration and Healing by Forgiving Myself**

Forgiving myself was hard. I carried guilt like a second skin—especially about my marriage ending and the impact on my children.

But my healing required compassion. I had to remind myself: I did the best I could with what I knew at the time. And now, I choose growth. I choose grace. I choose to honor the woman I was. I salute the woman I am today.

6. Restoration and Healing by Forgiving Others

Deep restoration and healing came by forgiving and freeing myself from the bondage of resentment. I wrote letters I never sent. I cried through prayers of release.

Compassion and forgiveness have been a gift to my spirit and soul, freeing me to live without any residue of bitterness or anger.

7. Restoration and Healing by Living a Purpose-Driven Life

As I healed, I began to rediscover the woman beneath the wounds—the one who had always been drawn to teaching, encouraging, and equipping others. With each step toward wholeness, my purpose became clearer: to help people grow personally, professionally, and spiritually.

This clarity led me back to the field of training and development, where I had once thrived. I returned to designing and delivering leadership and professional development programs—work I had first embraced during my military service and later at a grassroots nonprofit serving underserved adults. Even when my job titles didn't include "trainer," I found ways to weave learning and empowerment into every role I held. It was never just a job; it was a calling.

I also poured into my community. I led and continue to lead women's life groups at church, creating safe spaces for spiritual and personal growth. I teach courses at a local community college, helping students build personal skills.

Whether in classrooms, church groups, or small circles of support, I use my voice and my gifts to uplift others.

Living a purpose-driven life has been one of my greatest sources of healing. It reminded me that my pain had not disqualified me—it had prepared me. I wasn't just surviving anymore. I was serving, sowing, and shining in the spaces where I was called to make a difference.

8. Restoration and Healing by Shutting Down Toxic Relationship Patterns

The final exam of my restoration and healing came with my ability to effectively shut down toxic behaviors. I set boundaries and implemented consequences. I stopped explaining my worth. I stopped shrinking to fit someone else's comfort.

I choose relationships that feel safe, reciprocal, and nourishing. And as painful as it is, I release relationships with those who continue to disrespect and mistreat me and who do not honor the person I am today.

Your Invitation to Rise and Be Restored

Restoration and healing aren't my endpoints—they're daily acts of courage. Letting go of doormat behaviors isn't just about asserting myself; it's about honoring my truth. It's about finding my voice, embracing my joy, and stepping fully into my wholeness.

If you were inspired by my restoration and healing testimonies, know this: healing is possible. Restoration is real. And you, dear reader, are worthy of both.

Let this chapter be your invitation—to rise, to reclaim, and to restore.

Healing and Restoration Self-Reflection Questions

1. Which restoration and healing practices are you engaging in right now?

2. Which practices will you add to your restoration and healing process?

Chapter Eleven

Putting It All Into Action

Dr. Jermaine Hunter put in the work—steadily, courageously, and with unwavering commitment, applying action steps outlined in this book not as a checklist, but as a lifeline.

His journey from Wounded to Wisdom is not just a personal triumph. It's a living testimony to what's possible when we choose healing over hiding, growth over grief, and action over avoidance.

Through his story, readers will see how the actions come alive in real time, offering a blueprint for anyone ready to rise from the ashes of their own experience and walk boldly into a life of clarity, strength, and self-respect.

Dr. Jermaine's Story: Wounded to Wisdom

There came a point in my life when looking in the mirror became painfully difficult. I no longer recognized the person staring back. Physically, I saw myself and was mostly content with that version. But the part of me that couldn't be seen—my emotional core—was drowning in silent shame.

For years, I hid behind a mask shaped by toxic behaviors, convinced it would make me the most likable person in any room. And in some ways, it worked—people liked me. But not because I was whole or truly seen. They liked me because I made myself small, easy to overlook, and easy to use. I gave others the freedom to be fully themselves in our relationships while quietly abandoning my own need for authenticity and self-protection.

I was living in a wounded state of mind, one fueled by self-hate and emotional neglect. But within that woundedness came a moment of awakening: I decided I would no longer look in the mirror and not recognize who I was. If I wanted to be true to myself—both inside and out—something had to change.

By profession, I'm a risk manager—trained to analyze why events occur and identify what steps can prevent them from happening again. One day, it hit me: why not apply those same skills to myself? Why not investigate the "why" behind my doormat behaviors and transform them from sources of pain into lessons of wisdom and purpose?

That realization marked the beginning of my healing journey—guided by self-reflection, therapy, and a commitment to rediscovering the person I was always meant to be.

The Wounded Mirror

Any good mirror reflects who you are—and sometimes, how you came to be that way. When I looked into my own metaphorical mirror of hurt, I saw a lifetime of events that shaped my doormat behavior. But one moment stands out vividly to this day.

I was about eleven years old. It was a blistering summer afternoon. My best friend and I had been playing outside for hours, as kids often did back then. We were having the times of our lives when my parents pulled up to take us to the neighborhood store.

We piled into the car still soaked in summer heat. My mother immediately became agitated by the smell lingering on us. After a quick investigation, she discovered I'd forgotten to put on deodorant that day. Let's just say I wasn't the freshest person in the car!

For most parents, that would've been a simple, teachable moment—a gentle reminder to an eleven-year-old about the importance of daily hygiene. But for my mother, it became something far bigger. She saw it as the ultimate act of hygienic blasphemy and scolded me harshly—not just in front of my best friend, but also in front of my father, who had been mostly absent from my life until then.

That moment wounded me deeply. It stripped away my confidence and planted a fear of ever being seen as "less than." From that day forward, I wore the mask of perfection. I believed that to be accepted, I had to be flawless. If I weren't perfect, I wouldn't be valued. So, I began living from a place of performance rather than authenticity.

As I've grown and reflected, I've realized there were many moments like this—experiences with my mother and other significant figures that added layers to my mask. Back then, I didn't understand what was happening. I only knew I wanted to be loved and accepted, no matter the cost. If that meant silencing my true self, so be it. Because even conditional love and acceptance felt better than rejection.

When Hurt Becomes Habit

The longer I wore my masks—shaped by internal and external wounds—the easier it became to keep them on. Over time, they stopped feeling like disguises and started feeling like me, or at least who I thought I was. It's like the old saying: "If you tell a lie long enough, even the liar will believe it." I believed the versions of myself I had created, and that belief showed up in every area of my life—professionally, socially, and romantically.

I approached relationships with the mindset that I had to be likable for them to work. While being likable isn't inherently bad, neglecting my own worth and allowing others to cross my boundaries was deeply unhealthy. My doormat behavior taught people that it was acceptable to treat me however they pleased, as long as it made them feel good. They were free to be themselves, while I quietly absorbed their dysfunction and internalized it. Meanwhile, my confidence and self-worth steadily eroded.

At work, I often stayed silent about issues I knew were wrong for the organization or my team. I feared that speaking up would make me seem uncooperative. In friendships, I allowed selfishness to thrive and one-sided dynamics to persist. Rather than address the imbalance, I hid behind passive-aggressive behavior—most of which went unnoticed. In romantic relationships, I worked tirelessly to prove I was "the best guy they'd ever known." But because my efforts were driven by hurt and a desperate need for acceptance, I became easy to manipulate. My love turned into a daily performance—a relentless audition for someone else's approval.

It was exhausting. Yet it felt like my truth—even if that truth was a lie. For years, I lived in this self-made charade, smiling through the pain and calling it strength.

What Pain Taught Me

I've always been drawn to tattoos that tell a story—symbols etched in skin that reflect a person's life, pain, and growth. For me, the image of a crying clown captured how I moved through life: making others happy, sometimes entertaining their brokenness, all while concealing my own internal sadness.

While researching the perfect design, a profound question surfaced: "Who makes the clown smile?" That question sparked deep reflection about my own happiness and the progress I'd made through therapy.

For the longest time, I believed my therapist's role was to help me understand how my past hurt others. But I came to realize the real work began when I started understanding how my hurt allowed others to affect me. At first, focusing on my own healing felt selfish—until I remembered the instructions you hear on airplanes: "Put your oxygen mask on yourself first before helping others."

That realization revealed the answer to my question: the clown must create happiness from within. True happiness lives there. If we constantly look to others for our happiness, we risk letting others define us. And it's in that space that doormat behaviors are born and nurtured.

The Work Behind the Wisdom

Once I accepted that my happiness was my responsibility, I began the deeper work of restoration. Healing didn't happen overnight. It required intentional, layered effort—work I now see as sacred.

I committed to therapy not just to vent, but to excavate the roots of my pain. My therapist helped me trace patterns, but I had to do the heavy lifting: journaling, reflecting, and sitting with truths that were hard to swallow.

I sought feedback from trusted sources—people who loved me enough to be honest. Their insights revealed blind spots and challenged me to grow beyond my comfort zone. I practiced forgiveness—not only toward others, but toward myself. That was the most challenging part: releasing the shame of past choices and embracing the grace to begin again.

I rebuilt my self-awareness through daily reflection and mindfulness. I learned to name my emotions, honor my needs, and recognize when I was slipping into old patterns. I strengthened my self-esteem by celebrating small wins and affirming my worth—even when no one else did.

And perhaps most importantly, I developed assertiveness. I learned to speak up—not with aggression, but with clarity and self-respect. I stopped shrinking to make others comfortable. I stopped apologizing for existing.

This work—layered, intentional, and ongoing—is what turned my wounds into wisdom. It's what made me whole.

Living My Truth

Now that I know happiness begins within, I live by a simple but powerful truth: To be the best for you, I must first be the absolute best for myself.

With that mindset, I no longer shrink to fit in or seek validation to feel "enough." My worth is rooted in my wholeness. And that is where my doormat behaviors ended—and my true healing began.

Wounded to Wisdom Self- Reflection Questions

1. What aspects of Dr. Jermaine's story resonated with you?

2. How do you identify with Dr. Jermaine's story?

Chapter Twelve

Repairing the Damage from Doormat Behaviors

Releasing doormat behaviors began when I turned 40 and required years of reflection, learning, unlearning, and healing. I finally reached a place where saying no, speaking up, and shutting down disrespect became as natural as breathing. I reached a place where I could speak and walk with full confidence and authenticity.

With this accomplishment, I was ready and equipped to take on the responsibility of repairing the damage caused by years of being a doormat. This assignment was not small. It required the courage to permanently dismantle and rewrite toxic and generational patterns that had been normalized, tolerated, and passed down.

Repairing damage from doormat behaviors means taking the lead in facilitating the healing of open wounds in the workplace, in family, and in personal relationships. It means leading the shift from toxic dynamics to consistently healthy interactions. It means upholding standards of respect even when others resist. And perhaps the most powerful work of all is leading generational change—interrupting unhealthy patterns so the next generation inherits something better.

This chapter guides you through the courageous work of repairing the harm created by doormat behaviors. It is ongoing, honest, and deeply liberating work.

1. **Repair by Acknowledgement and Apologizing**

Toxicity rarely grows in isolation. It spreads in environments where silence becomes permission and where boundaries are absent or inconsistent. When you operate as a doormat, you unintentionally create fertile ground for unhealthy behavior to flourish.

Acknowledgment and apologizing are not about blaming yourself for someone else's mistreatment. Their choices are still their choices. It is about owning the ways your doormat behavior—avoiding conflict, absorbing disrespect, and minimizing your needs—played a role in sustaining the unhealthy relationship dynamic.

A sincere acknowledgment and apology might sound like:

- "I realize that by not speaking up, I allowed things to go on far longer than they should have."

- "I'm sorry for the resentment that built up because I didn't communicate my needs."

- "I apologize for the confusion my silence created."

This is not groveling. It is clarity. It is maturity. It is leadership. This step is powerful because it shifts you from a state of victimhood to one of agency. You cannot change what you refuse to acknowledge. You cannot change what you refuse to acknowledge.

2. Repair by Consistently Modeling Respect and Engagement Standards

People will test your new boundaries—not always out of malice, but out of habit. They want to know if this new version of you is real or temporary. Your consistency is proof.

Consistently modeling respect and engagement standards means:

- Speaking respectfully even when you're frustrated.
- Holding your boundary without over-explaining.
- Walking away from disrespect without drama.
- Following through on the consequences you've communicated.
- Treating others with the same dignity you expect.

When your behavior aligns with your words, the environment around you must shift.

3. **Repair by Leading Generational Change**

    Generational change is the deepest and most transformative layer of repair. It is where you interrupt family patterns and intentionally create new ones for those coming behind you.

    Leading generational change means:

    - **Naming the patterns out loud**

        You cannot heal what you refuse to name. You break generational cycles by shining light on what was previously unspoken.

    - **Modeling healthy behavior for the next generation**

        Family members learn more from what you consistently demonstrate than what you say.

Model healthy behavior by:

- speaking up respectfully

- walking away from chaos

- setting boundaries without guilt

- refusing to tolerate disrespect

- apologizing when needed

- holding others accountable

By doing this, you are teaching them a new way to exist in relationships.

- **Refusing to pass down emotional burdens**

You stop the cycle when you stop normalizing dysfunction. You stop the cycle when you stop absorbing mistreatment. You stop the cycle when you stop teaching others—through your silence—that their voice doesn't matter.

- **Creating new family norms**

  Generational change is not about perfection. It is about intention. It is about saying, "This stops with me," and then living in a way that makes that declaration true.

  Leading generational change is not just repairing your past; it is protecting your family's future.

4. **Repair by Telling Your Story**

   Your story is one of the most powerful tools you have for healing—both personally and generationally. When you tell your story with honesty, humility, and courage, you create space for others to reflect, grow, and choose differently.

   Telling your story means:

   - **Being transparent about where you started**

Share the moments when you stayed silent, overextended yourself, or accepted treatment that wounded your spirit. Not to relive the pain, but to show the truth of where transformation began.

- **Sharing what you learned along the way**

Your healing journey—your boundaries, your breakthroughs, your setbacks, your revelations—becomes a roadmap for someone else. Your story becomes evidence that change is possible.

- **Letting others see your humanity, not your perfection**

People don't connect to flawless stories. They connect to real ones. When you share your mistakes, your fears, and your growth, you model courage, not performance.

- **Using your testimony as a teaching tool**

Your story can interrupt generational silence. It can spark conversations your family has avoided for decades. It can help someone younger understand why you now choose peace over people-pleasing, clarity over confusion, and boundaries over burnout.

- **Showing the next generation what healing looks like in real time**

Your story becomes a living legacy. It becomes the bridge between what was and what can be. It becomes evident that cycles can be broken and rewritten.

When you tell your story, you are not exposing your wounds; you are exposing the path to healing. And someone in your family, your workplace, or your community will walk through a door you opened.

5. **Repair by Allowing Relationships to Recalibrate**

Repairing damage doesn't guarantee every relationship will survive the transition. Some people will rise to meet the new standard. Others will resist, resent, or retreat.

This is not failure. It is clarity. Healthy relationships will adjust. Unhealthy ones will reveal themselves.

Your job is not to force reconciliation. It is to maintain your integrity while allowing the natural recalibration to occur.

6. **Repair by Extending Yourself Grace**

As you lead the huge undertaking of repairing workplace, family, or personal relationships, you will not be perfect. You will fumble. You will overcorrect. You will say too much one day and not enough the next.

This is normal. Repairing damage from doormat behaviors is hard work, and there is no template for doing it perfectly. You deserve patience, compassion, and grace. Celebrate progress, not perfection.

The Detriments of Not Repairing the Damage in Organizations and Families

Failing to repair the damage caused by doormat behaviors doesn't keep the peace; it quietly deepens the wounds. When unhealthy patterns go unaddressed, they don't disappear. They spread. They harden. They become the unspoken rules that shape how people treat one another. Whether in a workplace or a family, unhealed relational damage becomes a breeding ground for toxicity.

In Organizations: When Silence Becomes the Culture

When doormat behaviors go unchallenged in the workplace, toxicity doesn't stay contained. It multiplies.

Unrepaired damage leads to:

- The spread of disrespectful or manipulative behavior.

- In-fighting and cliques that divide teams.

- Low morale and emotional exhaustion.

- High turnover as people leave to escape the dysfunction.

- Leaders lose credibility because they avoid addressing issues.

- A culture where the loudest or most aggressive voices dominate.

Workplace Example

Imagine a department led by a manager who routinely belittles employees, dismisses their ideas, and publicly shames anyone who makes a mistake.

Team members quickly learn that speaking up only invites more hostility, so they shrink themselves to avoid becoming the next target. No one challenges the behavior. No one defends one another. Everyone simply endures it.

Over time, silence becomes its own culture. Employees stop collaborating, creativity dries up, and people do only what is necessary to survive the day. The turnover rate climbs as the most capable and emotionally healthy employees quietly exit—not because they lack dedication, but because the environment is emotionally unsafe.

Despite the red flags—constant resignations, low morale, and repeated complaints— organizational leadership and employees who stay do nothing. The toxic manager remains in place, and the department continues to spiral. Productivity plummets, making it the lowest-performing unit in the entire organization. Yet the cycle continues, because no one is willing to confront and repair the root of the problem.

When you don't repair the damage, the workplace becomes a place where people survive, not a place where people thrive.

In Families: When Dysfunction Becomes Legacy

In families, unrepaired damage doesn't just affect the present; it shapes the future. When doormat behaviors and toxic dynamics go unaddressed, they become the blueprint for how the next generation learns to love, communicate, and resolve conflict.

Unrepaired damage leads to:

- Toxic behavior being passed down as "normal."

- Family members who don't know how to show love or respect.

- Emotional distance and resentment.

- Unhealthy communication patterns—silence, avoidance, or explosive conflict.

- Adult children going no-contact to escape the dysfunction.

- A family legacy built on survival instead of connection.

Family Example

Picture a family where one parent absorbs disrespect, avoids conflict, and keeps the peace at all costs. The children grow up watching one person shrink while others dominate. They learn that love means tolerating mistreatment or staying silent to avoid tension. As adults, some repeat the pattern in their own relationships. Others break away entirely, choosing distance over dysfunction. The family becomes fractured— not because they didn't care, but because no one ever repaired the damage.

When you don't repair the damage, the family becomes a place where wounds are inherited instead of healed.

Why Repair Matters for Your Future

When you understand the cost of leaving damage unrepaired—the fractured families, the toxic workplaces, the generational patterns that quietly repeat themselves—you begin to see why your healing work matters so deeply. Repair is not just a personal choice; it is a transformational act that reshapes environments, restores dignity, and rewrites legacies.

This is why the work you've done to release doormat behaviors is only the beginning. The next step is stepping forward with intention, courage, and clarity—choosing to build something healthier than what you inherited or tolerated.

And that brings us to the final movement of this chapter: the invitation to step boldly into a healthier future.

Stepping Into a Healthier Future

Repairing the damage from doormat behaviors is not about rewriting the past; it's about reclaiming your future and reshaping the legacy you leave behind. You are not defined by the patterns you once lived in. You are defined by the courage you show now.

When you acknowledge your part, apologize with humility, model your standards consistently, tell your story, allow relationships to recalibrate, and lead generational change, you create a new relational ecosystem—one rooted in dignity, clarity, and mutual respect.

This is the work of transformation. This is the work of healing. This is the work of becoming the person God always intended you to be, and the person future generations will thank you for becoming.

Chapter Thirteen

Conclusion

Throughout my adult life, I've read hundreds—perhaps thousands—of self-development books by credentialed experts. I am not one of them. I'm simply a person who has wrestled with behavioral patterns often addressed by therapists.

This book offers actions I used to release my doormat behaviors. I've chosen to authentically and vulnerably share my scars and struggles so that you might learn from my missteps and find your own path to growth. I am willing to lay myself bare in this way because my purpose is bigger than my comfort. I'm writing to reach those who are silently hurting—just as I once was.

Pain often hides behind polished smiles and polite nods. In a world that rewards division and disparagement more than connection and compassion, it's no wonder so many feel devalued. Can we really push through the noise, the distractions, and the dysfunction to do the deep work of healing?

I believe we can. I am living proof that transformation is possible.

Your Journey Through This Book

Let's take a moment to reflect on the ground we've covered:

- **Chapter 1:** Defined the metaphor "doormat" and set the stage for your journey.

- **Chapter 2:** Explored why people adopt doormat behaviors and what drives them.

- **Chapter 3:** Helped you assess whether this metaphor applies to your own experience.

- **Chapter 4:** Introduced six actions to release doormat behaviors.

- **Chapter 5:** Identified 12 common toxic relationship patterns and invited reflection.

- **Chapter 6:** Offered strategies to seek clarity, and support resources to consider.

- **Chapter 7:** Introduced eight strategies for setting boundaries and enforcing consequences with clarity and confidence.

- **Chapter 8:** Shared four personal growth areas that helped me release doormat behaviors.

- **Chapter 9:** Provided deep, thought-provoking questions to assess the viability of your relationships.

- **Chapter 10:** Shared my testimony of eight restoration and healing lifelines.

- **Chapter 11:** Presented Dr. Jermaine's powerful "Wounded to Wisdom" story and the actions he took to reclaim his life.

- **Chapter 12:** Guided you through the courageous work of repairing the harm created by doormat behaviors.

Depending on where you are in your journey, this book may feel overwhelming. But I want to offer you hope. When you move beyond allowing others to mistreat or disrespect you, when you stop saying yes when your soul is screaming no, and when you finally unmute your voice, you will be astonished by the shift. Your walk, your talk, and your very presence will change. You'll begin to experience joy, peace, and authenticity in ways that defy description. And I can't wait for you to feel it too.

So, take one step at a time. Choose actions that align with your personality and pace. Allow yourself time to grow, to stumble, and to rise again. Extend grace to yourself when old habits resurface. Extend grace to others when they fall short. This is not a race—it's a reclamation.

No Longer Your Doormat: A Practical Guide to Releasing Doormat Behaviors is not just a title— it's a declaration. Let it echo in your heart as you walk forward with courage. You are not who you used to be. You are becoming who you were always meant to be.

About the Author

Renee Gibbons is an educator, mentor, and advocate for personal and spiritual growth. For over 15 years, she has created and facilitated leadership and professional development programs across the federal and nonprofit sectors, helping hundreds build confidence, sharpen skills, and lead with purpose.

She has been leading Women's Life Groups at Zion Church for more than a decade, offering faith-based encouragement and practical wisdom. In addition, she serves as adjunct faculty at Prince George's Community College, empowering adult learners through accessible, growth-centered instruction.

Now retired, she devotes her time to writing, teaching, and community building. She lives in Upper Marlboro, Maryland, with her husband.

About the Contributor

Dr. Jermaine L. Hunter is a dedicated leader committed to service, safety, and empowering others to reach their full potential. With a strong background in Risk Management and Occupational Safety, he serves as Vice President of a major nonprofit organization, leading initiatives that create safe and equitable employment opportunities.

A proud member of Omega Psi Phi Fraternity, Inc., Dr. Hunter is passionate about mentoring, youth development, and uplifting his community. He also serves as an adjunct professor at Prince George's Community College (PGCC) and is a certified First Aid, CPR, and AED instructor.

Guided by faith and purpose, Dr. Hunter motivates others to lead, serve, and excel with integrity. In his free time, he visits his daughter at college and enjoys time with his two English bulldogs, Penny and Marley.